Infant Communication
Development, Assessment,
and
Intervention

Based on the National Symposium on Infant Communication sponsored by the Department of Communicology, College of Social and Behavioral Sciences, University of South Florida, and held March 5–7, 1981.

Infant Communication
Development, Assessment, and Intervention

Edited by

Dan P. McClowry, Ph.D.
Arthur M. Guilford, Ph.D.
Sylvia O. Richardson, M.D.

Department of Communicology
College of Social and Behavioral Sciences
University of South Florida
Tampa, Florida

GRUNE & STRATTON
A Subsidiary of Harcourt Brace Jovanovich, Publishers
New York   London
Paris   San Diego   San Francisco   São Paulo
Sydney   Tokyo   Toronto

Grune & Stratton, Inc.
111 Fifth Avenue
New York, New York 10003

Distributed in the United Kingdom by
Academic Press Inc. (London) Ltd.
24/28 Oval Road, London NW 1

Library of Congress Catalog Number 82-83122
International Standard Book Number 0-8089-1533-9

Printed in the United States of America

3-1303-00059-1918

3/12/54

*To Pauline, Dorothy, and Johanna
who gave us the inside story on infancy.*

Contents

Acknowledgments

The chapters presented here are based on papers presented at the symposium "Infant Communication: Assessment and Intervention," held on March 5–7, 1981, in Tampa, Florida. This conference was sponsored by the Department of Communicology, College of Social and Behavioral Sciences, and the Center of Life Long Learning, University of South Florida, Tampa, Florida.

This project would not be complete without mentioning at least some of the special people who contributed to various aspects of its development, from the attainment of funding through typing rough copy and proofreading final drafts. The funding for this project was obtained from Quality Improvement Funds allocated from the State of Florida to the State University System. Travis Northcutt, Dean, and Susan Stoudinger, Associate Dean, both of the College of Social and Behavioral Sciences, University of South Florida, and Stewart Kinde, Chairman, Department of Communicology, are greatly appreciated for their work in obtaining financial support for this project. Linda Lombardino and Nancy Harlan are recognized for their participation in panel discussions during the symposium. In addition, much appreciation is extended to Suzanne Daly for her suggestions and support throughout the planning stages of the conference.

Many individuals were very helpful during all aspects of the preparation of this manuscript. We gratefully acknowledge the time and effort contributed by the following: Terry Adams, Janis Frawley, Kim Galant, Lucia Grimaldi, Kelmie Hollahan, Cathy Johnson, Rose Kersey, Joanne Medeiros, Lori Norgart, Maureen Piscitelli, and Glenda Sullivan. Finally, there would have been no conference without the valuable contribution of our speakers. It is with much gratitude that we thank each of our contributors.

Preface

This book presents relevant and timely information covering communication development of the human infant. Specifically considered are dysfunction when developmental sequences are not met and methods for professional assessment of developmental delays seen in at-risk infants. Once problems areas have been identified, the professional must implement environmental planning and intervention to facilitate the infant's developmental skills.

This volume opens with an examination of the growth of the field of infant communication and the understanding of developmental delays in high-risk infants. Dr. Sylvia Richardson presents a historical perspective of intervention approaches with young children. She discusses the slow but steady progression of both interest in and programming for younger and younger children, to the current level of skill-based management of the newborn. Dr. Richardson's chapter presents the historical framework upon which we can develop new perspectives on the needs for future programming and planning for these infants.

In the second chapter, Dr. Dan McClowry and this author discuss the state of the art in current programming and provide a brief overview of recent changes in programming directed to assist communication development in infants. This chapter examines the functioning of the normal three-year old child and the developmental aspects of the infant as he or she progresses toward more skilled communicative functions. Future perspectives are explored and are further defined and developed in following chapters.

An infant's social and object skills are addressed by the presentation of a prototype assessment tool currently being developed and revised by Dr. Jeffrey Seibert and Anne E. Hogan. This tool, the *Early Social Communication Scales (ESCS)*, is presented in detail by its authors as they show the development of the theoretical issues relevant to this instrument. They focus specifically on the importance of early qualitative assessment of the infant's social and object skills and the significance of each to the communication process.

Play assessment as it relates to the development of prelinguistic behaviors is presented by Dr. Lorraine McCune-Nicolich. The author's substantial research supports the importance of play in a child's social, cognitive, and linguistic development. Procedures are detailed for systematic assessment of a child's play, including the selection of appropriate toys for use in assessment and for quantifying the child's developmental level of play. Dr. McCune-Nicholich provides suggestions for enhancing communication development through a systematic blending of play and language therapy.

An ecological model for language intervention in the developmentally delayed child is detailed in the chapter by Dr. James MacDonald. Communication strategies that are important for the child and significant other are presented. Of great importance to this approach is the shift in focus from a client-centered program to a unique clinician–client–significant other training program. In this innovative presentation, we discover the importance of the child's total environment. Emphasis is placed on the role of the significant other through interaction, assessment, modeling and intervention program training. The communication strategies as presented by Dr. MacDonald show the importance of dyadic social interaction for the development of form, content, and use.

Considerations for total programming for multihandicapped children are presented in a chapter by Philippa Campbell. Models of intervention for these children are related to her current program at Kent State University in which implementation of sensorimotor programming is being accomplished in a public school setting. Through the presentation of this clinical model, the author introduces a new team approach which has at its core both child and family needs. This chapter presents a model program that will be followed and imitated by many.

This volume concludes with consideration of a special training need. The importance of training and educating young school-aged parents of normal, at-risk, and multihandicapped children is addressed by Dr. Nicholas Anastasiow. He focuses on the increasing numbers of young parents and on the incidence in this population of high-risk or multihandicapped children. The educational system has provided only marginal training for these young parents, choosing at times to ignore or fail to recognize their special needs. This chapter identifies programs available to help these young parents and discusses the success of these programs in assisting young parents to develop their own parenting and life-coping skills.

The editors hope that this book will provide the catalyst for continued research, innovative problem solving, and the development of new intervention and assessment techniques for the developmentally delayed infant. *Infant Communication* presents the professional level of sophistication today and initiates plans for future developments. We are currently seeing the emergence of new technologies, refined skills, and total team programming. We are implementing effective problem-solving strategies for these infants and their families, while simultaneously planning for their future needs. We are in the midst of an exciting and innovative transition in programming for language delayed infants and are on the threshold of future developments.

Arthur M. Guilford, Ph.D.

Contributors

Nicholas J. Anastasiow, Ph.D.
Professor of Special Education
Hunter College
New York, New York

Philippa H. Campbell, O.T.R.
Coordinator, Community Outreach
Children's Hospital Medical Center of Akron
Akron, Ohio

Arthur M. Guilford, Ph.D.
Associate Professor of Communicology
Coordinator, Speech Language Pathology
College of Social and Behavioral Sciences
University of South Florida
Tampa, Florida

Anne E. Hogan
Graduate Fellow
Department of Psychology
University of Miami
Coral Gables, Florida

James D. MacDonald, Ph.D.
Associate Professor of Communication
Director, Parent–Child Communication Project
The Nisonger Center
Ohio State University
Columbus, Ohio

Dan P. McClowry, Ph.D.
Assistant Professor of Communicology
Director, Preschool Program
College of Social and Behavioral Sciences
University of South Florida
Tampa, Florida

Lorraine McCune-Nicolich, Ed.D.
Assistant Professor of Education
Douglass College
Rutgers University
New Brunswick, New Jersey

Sylvia O. Richardson, M.D.
Distinguished Scholar and Professor of Communicology
College of Social and Behavioral Sciences
Department of Pediatrics
School of Medicine
University of South Florida
Tampa, Florida

Jeffrey M. Seibert, Ph.D.
Assistant Professor of Pediatrics and Psychology
Mailman Center for Child Development
University of Miami
Miami, Florida

Infant Communication
Development, Assessment, and Intervention

HISTORICAL PERSPECTIVES

Sylvia O. Richardson
University of South Florida

When one considers that it is only within the last thirty years that preschool children have been considered interesting or even educable, it is indeed remarkable that today we are here to consider the study of infant communication. Notwithstanding the current stress on presentation of up-to-date information with relative disregard of its derivation, it seems appropriate to begin with a brief historical review of significant ancestors in the field.

For a long time there was belief in the myth that a child is a "tabula rasa," a clean slate or tablet on which the parents and society can inscribe ultimate behavioral patterns, a malleable mass to be shaped at will by the environment. Or it was believed that he was an homunculus, a rigid structure whose characteristics were fixed and unchangeable. These early beliefs have not been entirely eradicated, but they have been modified. Continuing emphasis on the effects of the social and physical environment on the development of the infant and child seems to be a derivative of the tabula rasa notion. Also, belief in the fixed IQ has been reminiscent of the homunculus notion.

Possibly one of the earliest and most remarkable trailblazers in the education of young children was Johann Amos Comenius (1592-1670), a Moravian Bishop, who recognized that improved education would result in improved social conditions. In his book, The Great Didactic, Comenius set forth his principles of education: (1) all instructions should be carefully graded and should be arranged to follow the order of nature; (2) the teacher should appeal to the understanding of the child through sense perception; (3) the teacher is to impart knowledge and to guide the memory; (4) the effective teacher goes from the known to the unknown in teaching children, and from the general to the specific; (5) subject matter should be selected for its usefulness, supported by concrete examples and frequent repetitions to fix ideas; (6) students should learn by observing and doing and by use rather than precept; (7) discipline for children

should be mild; and (8) early childhood education is important. Comenius set forth these principles 300 years ago,
and still much of his material concerning the education of
young children can be read profitably today by teachers and
parents. He even produced the first illustrated elementary
school textbook, Orbus Pictus.

About a hundred years later, Jean Jacques Rousseau
(1712-1778), a political writer interested in education,
stated in his book, Emile, that everything as it comes from
the hand of the Creator is good. He believed that everything became corrupt only in the hands of man. To Rousseau
the natural impulses of the child were inherently good and
he believed that expression rather than repression was a
fundamental tenet of education. In the early 18th century
this was considered revolutionary.

Among those most deeply influenced by Rousseau was
Johann H. Pestalozzi, a young German-Swiss educator (1746-
1826). Pestalozzi tried to formulate a teaching method
based on the natural development of the children, since he
believed that education should develop the child as a
whole--mentally, physically and morally. To do this, he
felt that education should follow the organic development of
the child, each step growing out of the preceding one.

Froebel (1782-1852), of German parentage, was deeply
impressed with the value of music and play in the education
of children that he observed in the school of Pestalozzi.
Froebel opened a school for small children in which he fea-
tured play, games and songs. He called this school the Kindergarten. Froebel gave additional emphasis to the idea
that education comes chiefly from doing, and, because he
recognized the value of play as an educational force in the
lives of children, play and games became a prominent feature
of his Kindergarten.

Perhaps the foremost American educational philosopher
of our time was John Dewey. The publication of his Demo-
cracy and Education in 1916 was a formidable event. Dewey
believed that the child's development is the sum total of
his reactions to the environment in which he lives. Education is a continuous reconstruction of the child's experiences. For Dewey, education was not to be considered a
preparation for life in the future but rather a continuing
process of living here and now.

Dewey, along with his predecessors, emphasized greatly the role of direct concrete meaningful experience in the education of the child. He saw that the child concentrates on and puts effort into only that which has genuine value or meaning for him. He found (as did Montessori) that no external force or reward becomes necessary to stimulate the child to learn if learning is allowed to arise from the normal experiences of the child.

Dewey emphasized the need for studying both the psychological nature of the individual and the social nature of the environment in which he lives. In the application of his principles to education, he pointed out that the child is an active being with natural impulses to communicate with others, to build and to construct, to investigate and to create. It is these impulses that the school should not only recognize, but employ actively in the process of education.

In all of these educators we see similar philosophies woven into the tapestry of educational theory: the importance of early education; the need for educational methods which will follow the maturational or neuro-physiological sequence of child development; the importance of the senses and of motor activity as basic to learning; that the child learns best by doing; and the tremendous importance of the environment from which the child must draw his experiences. These threads are also woven through the matrix of Dr. Maria Montessori's approach to education. However, she formulated a structured, systematic method of early education based on these principles.

Maria Montessori (1870-1952) (the first woman to receive a degree in medicine from the University of Rome) has had a tremendous influence on the education of young children. Yet she is rarely cited as the author or advocate of the large number of ideas and practices which are so characteristic of her teaching, and are now part of the early education scene in America. Dr. Montessori was strongly influenced by Rousseau and Pestalozzi, by Itard, a physician at the time of the French Revolution who became the father of Otolaryngology, and by Edward Seguin, who was the first person to provide a thorough educational system for mentally defective children. Seguin's book, Idiocy and Its Treatment by the Physiological Method, was published in New York in 1866. Montessori applied the principles of education propounded by Seguin to mentally defective children in Rome, during which time she also made her own modifications and amplified his theories until they were extended to the education of normal children.

Dr. Montessori describes the three major external features of her method as (1) the "prepared environment", (2) humility in the teacher and (3) the scientific ("sensorial") material. She prepared a pleasant environment where the children felt no constraint. In using this term, environment, she included:

> ...the whole assemblage of things from which the child is free to choose for using just as he pleases, that is to say, in conformity with his inclinations and his need for action. The teacher does nothing beyond helping him at first to get his bearing among so many different things, and to find out the precise use of them; that is to say, she initiates him into the ordered and active life of the environment. But after that she leaves him free to choose and carry out his work. (Montessori, 1965).

She believed that education should have as its object the development of independence in the child and frequently stated that "every unnecessary aid to a child is an impediment."

Of particular interest to us today, Montessori stressed the inner nature of all creativity, stating that creativity is best cultivated by concentrating first on the development of clear impressions and the consequent inner feelings associated therewith. Therefore, mastery of percepts and concepts is stressed.

Dr. Montessori's greatest contribution was in child psychology. She saw the child as totally separate and different from the adult; the child and adult representing two different forms of life. She had an inspiring respect, a reverence, for the child and his work. She taught that the child himself creates the man he is to become. Therefore, in order to prepare the appropriate environment for the child, we must come to understand the functions, purposes and needs of this busy little creature. She saw the child as a person in his own right, not as a miniature adult. She also saw the parents and the teacher as "directors," designers and custodians of the environment.

Concern over the education of children from three to six years of age blossomed in the 1960's. In 1965 there were many points of view among concerned professionals about the state of knowledge of how to prepare children for formal education. A few believed that the laws of early human development were well understood and that all that was needed was an effort to apply that knowledge. Richard Wolf, a colleague of Benjamin Bloom at the University of Chicago, expressed that point of view in a seminar at the Harvard Graduate School of Education. A few others either had been writing about the problems of disadvantaged preschool children or were actually operating experimental programs. Martin Deutsch and David Weikart were already operating compensatory preschool elementary programs. Deutsch stressed the problems of inadequate sensory discrimination (among other presumed deficits) while Weikart, who was less sure of what the root problem was, designed more eclectic programs.

Also in the sixties, Carl Bereiter was performing the first dramatically successful compensatory preschool program (Bereiter & Engelmann, 1966). Bereiter concluded that disadvantaged six-year-old children had deficiencies that were primarily cognitive and linguistic. He, therefore, devised a highly focused remedial curriculum that aimed at rapid improvement in those areas. His work was a form of educational engineering.

In addition to these pioneers in the field, numerous professionals had been working in the field of early education long before the problem of preschool education for the disadvantaged became fashionable. Shirley Moore, at the University of Minnesota; Barbara Biber, at the Bank Street College of Education; and Louise Bates Ames and Frances Ilg, at the Gesell Institute were some of the leaders of a large group of people who could justly be called "the establishment" in the field of early education. What these people believed about the total problem of early education is hard to say. They did apparently feel that they knew enough to train teachers and direct preschool education programs for middle-class three- to five-year-olds.

The 1960's also saw the development of preschool programs for children from low-income families. Such programs
were called "day-care" programs rather than nursery schools.
Day-care programs would look after young children for as
much as 10 hours a day while their parents worked, whereas
nursery schools usually operated on half-day basis. Many
day-care operators felt that they were preschool educators
while others claimed to provide only custodial care. This
group was not often consulted on the problem of early education and their views have never been fully heard.

The ranks of developmental psychology gave us J.
McVicker Hunt and Burton White who had been interested in
the role of early experience in human development for many
years. Hunt's interest covered the entire span of early
human development while White concentrated on the first six
months of life. Others such as Lewis Lipsitt at Brown
University, and Yvonne Brackbill at the University of
Florida, had been studying conditioning processes in infancy
and expressed a professional interest in the problem of
early education. Hunt and White were sure that society was
unprepared to cope immediately with the problem of compensatory early education. They shared the point of view that
early education for all children, not merely those judged to
be disadvantaged, was a societal goal of paramount importance. They also shared the view that the basic knowledge
about early human development, and especially about the role
of experience in development, simply was not available in
any but grossly inadequate amounts.

In 1971 Burton White embarked on a large project designed to generate knowledge about how best to rear children
during their first six years of life. He was concerned with
understanding the laws of optimal development. During the
course of this study, which is continuing, White and his
colleagues determined that the experiences of the second and
third years of life, and the performance of mothers during
that particular age period were of paramount importance.
One of their observations, relevant to effective child
rearing practices, is very pertinent to our discussion here:

"these (effective) mothers rarely spend five, ten,
or twenty minutes teaching their one or two-year-
olds, but they get an enormous amount of teaching
in 'on the fly,' and usually at the child's insti-

gation. Though they do volunteer comments oppor-
tunistically, they mostly act in response to
overtures by the child," (White, 1971).

The studies of innate temperamental attributes by
Thomas, Birch and Chess, begun in 1956 and still ongoing,
have been of enormous value in initiating the most recent
considerations of ways in which the infant or child influences his world. In their earliest report in 1963 we read:

"when parents learn that their role in the shaping
of their child is not an omnipotent one, guilt
feelings may lessen, hostility and pressure may
tend to disappear, and positive restructuring of
the parent-child interaction can become possible."
(Thomas, Birch & Chess, 1963).

From my point of view, the alleviation of parental
feelings of fear and impotence produced by guilt could be
the most important by-product of current exploration of the
reciprocal dynamics of the parent-child interrelation. This
is appropriate intervention--to come between and to alleviate negative parental thoughts and actions which can prevent
optimum care giving. The term intervention is somewhat
frightening because it does mean "to come between." Hopefully no studies, techniques or methods will come between
the parent and child.

Historically, our best approaches to child care and
guidance have come from intelligent and meticulous observations of infant and child behavior. We must learn to attend
selectively. We must continue to be led by the child.

REFERENCES

Bereiter, C., & Engelmann, S. Teaching disadvantaged children in the preschool. Englewood Cliffs, N.J.: Pren-
tice-Hall, 1966.

Thomas, A., Birch, H.G., Chess, S., et al. Behavioral indi-
viduality in early childhood. New York: New York University Press, 1963.

Montessori, Maria. Dr. Montessori's own handbook. New
York: Schocken Books, 1965.

White, B. L.   Human infants: Experience and pyschological
     development.   Englewood Cliffs, N.J.:   Prentice-Hall,
     1971.

2

NORMAL AND ASSISTED COMMUNICATION DEVELOPMENT

Dan P. McClowry   Arthur M. Guilford
University of South Florida

Miraculous as it seems, most children in just three or four years develop the basic phonological, semantic, syntactic and pragmatic skills that they need to engage in simple adult-like conversations. A typical three year old has acquired nearly four-fifths of the speech sounds heard in his environment, yet, he may be heard to ask for "anudder piece of birfday cake." He has mastered most of the rules for sequencing sounds into words and sentences, yet, he refuses to eat his mother's "puhsketti."

By age three, this toddler has amassed an expressive vocabulary of over 900 words. Due in part to his extensive travels through televisionland, his semantic dictionary has entries ranging from abominable snowman, backgammon, and capsule, to Xanadu, yogurt, and Zeus. Of course, his definitions may only slightly resemble those of the adult.

He is able to share his knowledge of the world by generating all of the basic sentence patterns and many more complex structures. "I go Grandma's farm." "Pap pap milk a cow." "I got sick." "Jimmy laugh." "Him gonna get a spanking." "The door is open, so I can get in." "Why don't mama do one?" "I'll show her how." "I think he'll play on the swings." His language is rich in its use of early developing morphological inflections such as present progressive, plurals, irregular past tense, uncontractible copula, articles, and possessive markers. He has the tools to send an unlimited number of messages.

This three year old can use his language in many ways. He seeks information, describes his trip to the beach, protests a playmate's use of his favorite toy, requests assistance in opening a jar of peanut butter, and answers the questions of others. His language is far from complete, yet, he is much advanced from the neonate whose expressive repertoire is basically reflexive.

His transformation from a reflexive to a socio-linguistic being occurs rapidly and apparently effortlessly. This process of communication development is easily taken for granted by most parents and professionals unless something in the process goes wrong. Some children may show delayed, deviant, or arrested language development. They may show regressed language skills, or may fail to develop the conventional communication system. Some may be mentally retarded, hearing impaired, or suffer from severe emotional problems. Developmental delay, environmental circumstances, or central nervous system dysfunction may affect their language development.

Communication problems may be manifested in a variety of ways with some children failing to develop the speech or articulatory aspect of their communication system due to apraxia, dysarthria, developmental delay or emotional problems. They may perform as though they are mute, while others, though loquacious, use idiosyncratic speech requiring that the rest of the world learn their sound system. Difficulty in sequencing speech sounds or paralysis which precludes speech production may affect some children. Some of these children may be similar to their talking peers in that they have much to say, but different, in that they have no way to say it.

Sequencing words into meaningful sentences and failure to acquire the rules for formulating complex sentence structures characterize a major communication problem for other children. These children may perform more fluently at the single word level or when relying on contextual cues to help them relate a series of meaningful units. They may use the semantically based grammar of young children to express their ideas. For these children with syntactic difficulties and those with articulation problems, the mastery of form seems to be the missing link to successful language development.

Another communication problem is apparent when children fail to develop an understanding of the relationships among objects or between people and objects. Failing to develop an understanding of objects in their world, they may have little to talk about. These children may not relate to objects from an adult perspective because of a failure to identify with others, that is, they may fail to see the significance of socially defined object functions. Retarded or delayed cognitive funcioning may be indicated for some of

these children.   In either case, it is the content area of
language development that is critically involved.

In contrast, other children who are experiencing difficulty developing communication may have a rich vocabulary
and adequate articulatory skills, but have no reason to
communicate. They find little reinforcing about the social
give-and-take of the communicative process. They may find
few external events reinforcing and those that are may be
events or behaviors that many would consider bizarre, dis-
tasteful, unproductive or pointless. More often than not,
these children show multiple problems involving the interaction of form, content, and use (Bloom and Lahey, 1978).

Distinctions among the communication problems of young
children may appear more clearly defined in print than in
reality. For example, there may be a tendency for some
speech/language clinicians to approach a form/modality
problem as if it represented expressive language delay.
Clinicians should be reticent to assign the label of expressive language delay to a child who is not talking, yet
showing adequate receptive language development. As Bloom
and Lahey (1978) and McLean and Snyder-McLean (1978) suggest, expressive and receptive language skills are approximately equal except during initial stages of language acquisition. Frequently, we find that the low expressive child
has a significnat form/modality problem that is independent
of language. Our data show that many of these children make
minimal progress when the focus of training is on the development of the semantic-grammatical aspects of expressive
language. Maximal gains occur when the focus of therapy is
on facilitating the form of expressing meanings by augment-
ing communication through signs or by supporting oral/motor
training with visual, tactile and kinesthetic cueing.

There also may be the tendency among some clinicians to
treat the child with seriously delayed expressive language
as a client with articulation problems and spend thousands
of trials attempting to get the child to make the "Sammy
snake" sound or the "whistling wind" sound when the child's
primary problem is lack of expressive language. Most probably these children initially will show a high rate of unintelligible speech as they learn to extend their knowledge of
semantic relationships and begin to increase the mean length
of their utterances. However, rarely is the child's articu-

lation so poor that those significant others in his environment fail to understand his intentions in the contexts of
familiar family routines or within low or high structured
home-based language stimulation activities.

Prelinguistic Development

Many children with communication problems show disturb-
ances in the development of social and cognitive skills in
infancy. Therefore, the clinician needs to become aware of
the aspects of sensorimotor development which are prerequisite to the acquisition of form, content, and use. As these
domains of communication develop synergistically, what is
prerequisite to one area will most likely affect the development of the other two. Infants and young children will
tend to use what is established in two domains as a stepping
stone to further develop the third. Slobin (1973) has
indicated that children will utilize new forms (words,
structures) to relate old content (familiar ideas, concepts)
for routine uses (functions or purposes).

Most sensorimotor behaviors show aspects of each communication domain, either explicitly or implicitly. This
perspective is most important when clinicians consider the
at-risk infant or profoundly involved older clients. The
clinician needs to develop sensitivity to what the child
brings to interpersonal transactions and build from his
base. For example, the child may show undifferentiated
action (form, but unconventional) in the presence of a
specific object (content) in order to get someone to repeat
an activity with the object (use). In this circumstance,
the clinician may select to target the shaping of a more
recognizable sign (conventional form) to indicate his already established use (request action) with respect to
familiar content.

The birth cry may be a prime example of the implicit
blending of form, content and use. The child initiaties the
social exchange as a naive participant, yet a message is
clearly received by his mother. She hears his cry and may
perceive any of the following messages:

Form	Content	Use
Cry	"Here I am."	Announcement
Cry	"I'm alright."	Reassurance
Cry	"I need you."	Request

This interaction is not to imply that the child has actually shown intentional communication; yet, how the mother interprets and responds to her baby's cry is integral to their bonding process.

In these relatively simple beginnings, the infant and his caregiver interact reciprocally, influencing each other's strategies for initiating, maintaining and terminating communication sequences (Seibert and Hogan, this volume). At times, the infant orchestrates the interaction by cueing his caregivers to adjust the timing, intensity and duration of their messages. As evidenced in these behaviors, the child presents a biological readiness for language development and through dynamic interactions with the social and object worlds his language emerges. It is shaped and augmented and gradually takes on the features of adult-like language. The child and his environment are active partners in the learning process.

Significance of Interactions with Objects

Inasmuch as language is used to present an individual's internalized "meanings" of environmental objects and events, it is imperative that we take a closer look at how these meanings develop. In a recent publication, McLean, Snyder-McLean, Jacobs and Rowland (1981) present a sequential description of semantic development. At the earliest level, the infant reacts to environmental stimuli through reflexive or other innate behavioral responses. He may show a startle reaction to a loud sound or to a change in his visual field. These primitive responses to novel stimuli are differentially reinforced either externally or internally, thus insuring further elaboration of his response repertoire. Later, the infant will begin to apply indiscriminately his primitive action schemes such as banging, mouthing, or shaking objects he encounters. For example, in neutral contexts, he is as likely to bang a toy as to mouthe it.

With continued experiences, the infant begins to accommodate to specific characteristics of the objects he encounters. Some objects roll, some stack, others produce sounds when shaken. As a result of acting on and observing actions on objects in social contexts the infant will gradually begin to use them in adultomorphic ways. For example, he will put the comb to his hair, the cup to his mouth, and place blocks in a can. The child begins to adopt conventional forms for representing the object world.

Soon, he will begin to coordinate action schemes into simple routines. He may dial the telephone while holding the receiver to his ear or feed the baby and put it to bed. Also, at this time he may begin to use objects as tools in problem solving. He may pull the tablecloth to obtain objects which are out reach or he may use the doll to knock down the tower of blocks.

We begin to see evidence that his use of objects in social situations reflects an underlying understanding of basic pragmatic functions and semantic notions. Bates, Camaioni and Volterra (1977) view the infant's use of objects to gain adult attention as proto-declarative and the infant's use of adults to obtain objects or to make something happen as proto-imperative. Bruner (1978) suggests that human action involves people performing actions on objects at some point in time. Likewise, the infant in his play activities indicates nonvocally that you not he will open the door; that you will throw the ball and not roll it; and that you are to drink the water not pour it. The infant's play with objects is rich in its reflections of his internal organization of the world. It reveals his understanding of the basic concepts of agent, action, object, instrument, location and time.

Significance of Interactions with People

Adult caregivers play a critical role in the infant's development of language. As MacDonald (this volume) emphasizes, the social exchanges between caregiver and infant form the matrix through which the infant will obtain his information about the reciprocal nature of conversation, the conventional forms that are used to transmit messages, and the objects and events which will comprise the content of his messages. McLean, et. al., (1981) have focused our attention on two significant socio-communicative developments: intentionality and dyadic interaction.

Initially, infant behaviors are reflexive; however, caregivers tend to react to them as if they were intentional. As a result, caregivers help the infant develop a greater interest in specific aspects of his environment. At times, the infant seems to focus all of his energies on such goals as reaching for an object or trying to make something happen. He does this without regard to his caregiver. Still, it is the adult who responds as if the child had intended to say "I want that" or "I want that to happen again." By seven to nine months, the infant will show an awareness that the caregiver is responding to him. His behaviors may be similar to those he produced earlier, however, at this time, his focus is shared with referent and caregiver. Through repeated experiences in routine contexts the infant's behaviors will begin to approximate conventional signs as he waves good-by, extends his hand for more, and raises his arms above his head to be picked up. Each of these nonlinguistic behaviors effectively conveys the infant's specific intentions at a given moment.

The infant's expressions of intentionality begin to acquire conventional forms as a result of their development within dyadic interactions. In daily verbal or nonverbal interactions, one partner initiates, the other responds. The response of the second person then sets the stage for a response from the person who initiated the communication sequence; thus, interaction begins, is maintained, and eventually is terminated. Any given interaction may involve a number of these exchanges resulting in a communication chain. McLean, et. al., (1981) identify two critical skills that are involved in the development of dyadic interaction or turntaking. First, the infant must learn to inhibit his responses in order to allow time for his communication partner to respond. Then, he must learn his role as a facilitator of "conversation"; he must recognize his turn, and formulate and produce an appropriate response to complete his link in the chain of communication.

As the infant becomes more interactive with family members, he will gain greater awareness of how vocalizations

effect change in the environment. He may begin by using
idiosyncratic "words" to request objects or events. Caregivers tend to reinforce these productions leading him to
more sophisticated forms of communication. By 11 to 14
months, the infant will begin to use conventional forms to
reference family members, pets, toys, and favorite foods.
When he attains this level, the infant seeing his father
will say "Daddy" or seeing mom with his cup will request
"juice." Soon he will begin to use two words in close
temporal proximity. For example, he may say, "Down...baby"
following his observation of a doll tumbling from the
clothes basket. Later, his sequences will become conventional and he will say "baby down," "drink juice," and "want
eat more cracker."

Impact on Intervention

The perspective of describing a child's communication
development in terms of the quality of his interactions with
people and objects has been particularly fruitful for clinicians working with developmentally delayed infants and young
children (Seibert and Oller, 1981). It has revolutionized
our approach to diagnosis and treatment. Clinicians are
finding that the division between assessment and intervention has been artificial. It is impossible to follow the
traditional model in which an individual is seen for an
initial observation and evaluation session, and then, on the
basis of test results, formulate an appropriate program that
may be carried out by another agency. The essence of communication development decries this approach.

Assessment/intervention is an ongoing process that is
as dynamic as the communication process itself. It provides
the description of how infants and their caregivers are
communicating within natural contexts. It seeks to determine how to highlight certain features of the communication
process to best elicit differential responses from the
infant. Assessment/intervention also focuses on the needs
of the infant's caregivers to help them learn to produce
dynamic disequilibrium in the environment to facilitate
greater infant responsivity. Additionally, it will teach
them to respond differentially to their infant's preinten-
tional and early communicative behaviors in order to establish bridges to higher levels of communicative functioning.

In the past ten to fifteen years, a number of researchers have designed procedures to facilitate the development of delayed infants and young children. Bronfenbrenner's (1974) review of early intervention programs showed that those programs which maintained gains over the primary years were those which included components of parental involvement. Other approaches which focused on training children within a clinical setting showed initial gains on some developmental tasks, but these gains deteriorated in the early elementary years.

Another approach reporting success across developmental areas in infants is the Milwaukee Project (Heber, Garber, Harrington & Hoffman, 1972). Participants in this project were children of mentally retarded mothers who were removed from the home for most of their waking hours. The program had no input into the home environment; however, this program followed a natural model for language stimulation. Each infant participating in this program was seen individually by the same 'teacher' for the first 12 to 15 months. Through this one-to-one interaction, bonding between child and 'teacher' occurred. Additional gains of this project included remarkable increases in the children's IQs. When control and experimental children were compared at age five and a half, the mean IQ score for the experimental group was thirty points higher, with a mean of 121 for this group.

McLean and Snyder-McLean (1978) have reviewed and critiqued various approaches to early language training. Among those reviewed was the Environmental Language Program (MacDonald, 1978) which they feel demonstrates fine examples of instrumental teaching contexts. They indicate that MacDonald's program focuses on language development from a child's perspective and strongly reflects the cognitive and social bases of language. MacDonald (this volume), recognizing the need for continued program development and refinement in the areas of conversation development and pragmatics, has extended his program through the development of the ECO. As seen in Chapter Five of this volume, he may well have developed one of the most pervasive programs available for addressing the critical aspects of evolving functional communication systems.

Implications

Language intervention programs continue to be developed and elaborated as clients demonstrate needs and clinicians and researchers respond with possible solutions. Traditionally, we followed an adult model as we developed therapeutic goals and procedures. At the height of the semantic revolution, our clinical programs reflected a child-based perspective, yet maintained the clinical model of one-to-one, stimulus-response transactions. Today, resting on a rich foundation of information regarding ecological theory, we begin to question the context of language training specifically as it relates to programs of assisted-language development for infants and young children.

One question to be considered is, can a "normal" environment make salient those aspects of language development which have been alluding the handicapped or at-risk infant? If the child is in an "atypical" environment, another question needs to be asked. Would moving toward a more normalized environment facilitate language development? These are pressing questions for parents and clinicians. When fully explored, they may lead to major changes in effective programming for handicapped children.

We know that with earlier recognition of at-risk infants and more effective programming, prognoses have never been better. With additional answers being sought through research, on-going clinical work, and followup, the future may be even brighter for our clients. When we can address total environmental planning, we will have begun to achieve our goal of establishing effective programs of assisted-communication development for the at-risk infant. Steadily, we have gained, and we will continue to gain new insights as we problem-solve to maximize the effectiveness of early intervention programs.

REFERENCES

Bates, E., Benigni, L., Bretherton, I., Camaioni, L., & Volterra, V. From gesture to the first word: On cognitive and social prerequisities. In M. Lewis & L. Rosenblum (Eds.), Interaction, conversation and the development of language. New York: Wiley and Sons, 1977.

Bloom, L. & Lahey, M. Language development and language disorders. New York: Wiley & Sons, 1978.

Bronfenbrenner, U. A report on a longitudinal program (Vol. II): Is early intervention effective? DHEW Publication Number (OHD) 74-24, 1974.

Bruner, J. Learning how to do things with words. In J. Bruner & A. Garton (Eds.), Human growth and development. Oxford: Clarendon Press, 1978.

Heber, R., Garber, H., Harrington, S., & Hoffman, C. Rehabilitation of Families at Risk for Mental Retardation. Madison, Wis: Rehabilitation Research and Training Center in Mental Retardation. University of Wisconsin, December, 1972.

MacDonald, J. Environmental language intervention program. Columbus: Charles E. Merrill, 1978.

McLean, J. & Snyder-McLean, L. A transactional approach to early language training. Columbus: Charles E. Merrill, 1978.

McLean, J., Snyder-McLean, L., Jacobs, P., & Rowland, C. Process-Oriented Educational Program for the Severely/ Profoundly Handicapped Adolescent. Bureau of Child Research. University of Kansas. Parsons Research Center. October, 1981.

Seibert, J. & Oller, K. Linguistic pragmatics and language intervention strategies. Journal of Autism and Developmental Disorders. Vol. II, 75-88, 1981.

Slobin, N.I. Cognitive prerequisites for the development of grammar. In C.A. Ferguson & D.I. Slobin (Eds.), Studies of child language development. New York: Holt, Rinehart & Winston, 1973.

3

A MODEL FOR ASSESSING SOCIAL AND
OBJECT SKILLS AND PLANNING INTERVENTION

Jeffrey M. Seibert and Anne E. Hogan
University of Miami

Language is complex and multifaceted. Its development remains far from fully understood. Nevertheless, the language practitioner has accepted responsibility for facilitating its acquisition in language-delayed children. We contend that, to be most effective, the practitioner needs a model of language that represents the processes underlying its development as best as they are currently understood. At a minimum, the model should provide the practitioner with good observational categories to describe the child's language-related behaviors and it should suggest probable developmental change mechanisms that may be translated into intervention strategies. In other words, the model should reflect the complexity of the processes it attempts to describe and facilitate.

Some available language models used to guide intervention, such as those derived from behavioral theory, appear to underestimate the complexity of the linguistic domain, which may in part account for their ineffectiveness. The behavioral model's analysis of language, only at the level of observable behavior and function, and its reliance primarily on imitation and reinforcement to foster change, may not be wrong, but it certainly is incomplete. Such an approach lacks the developmental detail needed by the practitioner to determine how and where to intervene in the language acquisition process. A more complex model is needed. However, complexity must not be invoked at the cost of practicality. Despite the behavioral approach's inadequacies, a definite appeal has been its relative simplicity, making its widespread implementation feasible. Complex models are fine for the theorist but the practitioner needs something that can be easily applied. A balance therefore needs to be struck between theoretical complexity and simplicity of application.

We will describe a model to guide the practitioner concerned with the development of prelinguistic and very early language skills, from birth to approximately two years of age. The model is based on a more general framework

(Fischer, 1980) that also has been applied to later language acquisition (e.g., Fischer & Corrigan, in press). The model proposes a complex analysis of language-related behaviors into a number of different categories. However, the model also proposes a basis for synthesizing the categories into a coordinated whole that gives an overall simplicity to the model. It is the combination of analysis with synthesis that should provide the necessary balance between complexity and simplicity to make the model practical. A model which attempts only to describe the complexity of language development through an analysis of the linguistic domain into a large number of categories and leaves the process of synthesis or reintegration of the categories to the practitioner may leave the practitioner overwhelmed by details. If, however, the model focuses on the total child and emphasizes interrelationships among the categories in terms of the child's overall functioning, the details should provide a finer focus for the total picture rather than obscure it. Whether the proposed model achieves the desired balance between complexity and simplicity remains to be evaluated by the practitioner in the field.

The General Framework

The general framework suggests a division of language-related issues and assumptions into two areas. The first of these includes linguistic assumptions. The second includes cognitive assumptions.

Linguistic assumptions. Language is commonly broken down into four areas for study: phonology, semantics, syntax, and pragmatics. It has been the more recent study of linguistic pragmatics that has had the greatest implications for the language practitioner (Miller, 1978; Rees, 1978; Seibert & Oller, 1981). Pragmatics is the study of the functions of language in context and how language enables the individual to achieve goals and affect the behavior of others. A pragmatic orientation to language development can serve an important synthesizing function in organizing one's perceptions of language-related behaviors. Effective communication and its development are the central issues. From this perspective, the focus of phonology, semantics, and syntax shifts to the study of the tools of effective communication. Specifically, phonology becomes the study of parameters of the physical channels through which communication is accomplished, semantics becomes the study of the meaning system available to the individual for communicative purposes, and syntax becomes the study of rules the individual has for combining words to communicate effectively about a wide range of complex topics.

The framework's pragmatic orientation suggests a basis for functional continuity between prelinguistic and linguistic development. It has been repeatedly demonstrated that the child is capable of intentional, directed communication prior to development of a language system, through his use of gestures, eye contact, and vocalizations (e.g., Bates, Camaioni & Volterra, 1975; Bruner, 1975a, 1975b; Bullowa, 1979; Hubley & Trevarthen, 1979; Sugerman-Bell, 1978). The assumption is that linguistic communication has its ontogenetic roots in a variety of prelinguistic skills and that they provide a foundation for the emergence of language. Furthermore, a search for the origins of prelinguistic communication skills in more primitive behaviors in turn becomes a concern of the practitioner.

Cognitive assumptions. The general cognitive orientation complements the framework's pragmatic approach, for at least two reasons. Effective communication, the focus of pragmatics, requires knowledge and problem-solving skills. Such topics are typically included in the study of cognition. In addition, the shift from prelinguistic to linguistic communication, a legitimate area of study for pragmatics, also represents a transition from nonsymbolic to symbolic communication (e.g., Morehead & Morehead, 1974). Symbolic development has traditionally been regarded as a cognitive concern. Therefore, a cognitive developmental analysis is needed to provide a complete description of developmental processes underlying language development.

The cognitive developmental assumptions are derived primarily from the neo-Piagetian theory of cognitive skill development proposed by Fischer (1980). The model defines cognition broadly to include the control of social skills focused on people, as well as traditional cognitive skills focused on objects. Cognition does not precede language nor does language provide the basis for thought. Rather language, as a set of social skills, is considered to be a subset of cognition. The important question concerns determining the relationship of specific language skills to other cognitive skills, such as traditional Piagetian sensorimotor skills. This question will be addressed later.

The framework proposes that domains be analyzed into task sequences or developmental dimensions. Some developmental sequences are invariant. Other sequences are not necessary but represent the order in which a set of skills is typically acquired. Invariant sequences in the development of skills occur only: 1) where one skill is a component of a second skill; 2) within narrow task sequences where changes in the stimulus conditions are minimal while the response to the situation is developing through a series of levels of increasing complexity (e.g., the development from simple, indiscriminate, repetitive actions with objects, such as banging and waving, to appropriate or functional use of the same objects); 3) where the same response must be given to increasingly complex stimulus dimensions of a task (e.g., locating an object that is hidden in an increasingly more complicated fashion).

According to the framework, many reported developmental sequences are not invariant but represent only the most typically observed order of acquisition. The following sample illustrates how this can happen. Two tasks may be of equivalent difficulty, so synchronous mastery would be expected. However, if most children typically have more opportunities for experience with the components and materials of one of the tasks, that task will most always be mastered before the second task. The two tasks may appear in an invariant order, yet the first is not prerequisite to the second and the order is only typical, not necessary.

Cognitive developmental theory (Fischer, 1980) hypothesizes that progress in the development of cognitive skills across domains can be characterized as passage through a fixed series of levels or stages of increasingly complex organizational structure. The structural level of functioning that a child manifests in any specific task sequence will depend on two factors: 1) his optimal level of performance, a cognitive limit probably imposed at any point in development by neurological factors reflecting maturation, and 2) his experiences with the conditions and materials relevant to the tasks in question. Lack of relevant experience can produce unexpected gaps in an individual's behavioral repertoire, regardless of his optimal cognitive developmental level. The explicit role attributed by Fischer's theory to experience in skill acquisition is used to account for decalages (differential rates in the acquisition of skills) that should emerge simultaneously because they are at the same developmental level (Fischer, 1980). Different information processing demands of similar but not identical tasks are factors that also may affect the relative rates of acquisition of related skills. Although such unevenness in the development of related skills has in the past been considered a serious challenge to Piaget's stage theory of cognitive development, Fischer's theory suggests that such asynchronies should be the rule rather than the exception.

The interesting implication of the cognitive structural assumption for our analysis of prelinguistic and linguistic communication skills is that it suggests that cognitive skills with objects and cognitive skills with persons share a common underlying organization. If that organization can be understood, it should provide the basis for viewing the child's development in what seem to be unrelated areas within a single integrative system. The complex array of categories produced by the analysis of domains into dimensions is reduced by viewing behaviors encompassed by the different categories from the perspective of shared structural levels.

In summary, the general framework of our model examines language-related developments from a pragmatic perspective, focusing on effective communication as the goal of intervention. Syntax, semantics and phonology become tools employed in the service of communication. Communication occurs prelinguistically as well as linguistically, suggesting a need for an analysis of the origins of communication in prelinguistic developments. The pragmatic focus on communication and language use suggests the need for a concurrent cognitive developmental analysis. The general cognitive-developmental assumptions are derived from Fischer (1980). Cognition is defined broadly in terms of the control of social as well as object-focused skills, and so includes aspects of language development. Fixed or invariant developmental sequences of skills are hypothesized to occur only where one skill is clearly a component of another skill; few observed developmental sequences are true invariant sequences. A series of cognitive levels should under-

lie most developmental skill sequences; skills from different domains are assumed to share a similar underlying cognitive organization. However, the child may not perform at
the same level of complexity in two different task sequences; his performance in each depends on whether he has
had the relevant experience to acquire the skills at the
same level in each task sequence. Unevenness in the development of skills at the same cognitive level becomes the
rule rather than the exception, unless opportunity for
experience has been controlled. Finally, because dissimilar
domains share common underlying levels of organization, the
concept of cognitive levels provides a basis for reintegrat-
ing the results of the analysis into a single framework.

The Model for Prelinguistic and Early Language Development

The proposed model applies principles of the general
framework, first through an analysis of the object and
social domains into task sequences or developmental dimensions, to generate a set of assessment scales for each
domain. Following this, the hypothesized cognitive levels
that characterize the developmental period from birth to two
years are described. Finally, a synthesis of the components
generated by each of these analyses is proposed.

In considering the object domain, recall that one
assumption of the general framework is that object skills
should be necessary for communication development only to
the extent that they are components of the communication
skills. A complete description of the specific links between skills in these two domains is beyond the scope of
this chapter; nevertheless, some aspects of the relationship
will be noted.

An analysis of the object domain. Uzgiris and Hunt
(1975), based on Piaget's theory and description of sensorimotor development, have developed a set of scales that
analyzes cognitive skills, primarily with objects, of the
first two years into multiple developmental dimensions. We
have adapted their scales to provide a focus on social
skills (Seibert & Hogan, 1979). Because their book provides
a very complete discussion of the origins and development of
their scales, we will describe each only briefly and note
research findings of possible relevance to communication
development.

The Development of Visual Pursuit and the Permanence of Objects assesses the child's developing capacity to maintain perceptual contact with an object that undergoes various transformations, ranging from displacement through space to occlusion of the object behind or under screens and inside containers. Its primary hypothesized connection to communication has been as an index of the general representational or symbolic capacity that underlies the symbolic use of language to refer to objects (Bloom, 1973). In general, research has failed to establish any strong relationship between object permanence and communication/language measures (Bates, Benigni, Bretherton, Camaioni & Volterra, 1979; Corrigan, 1976; Synder, 1978; Zachry, 1978). Corrigan (1977) has reported that the onset of one-word utterances and the onset of stage 6 object permanence occurred at about the same time in her sample and that success on the highest level object permanence task precedes emergence of words for recurrence ("more") and non-existence ("all gone").

The Development of Means for Achieving Desired Environmental Events examines the child's ability to use his own body and object intermediaries to obtain goals (desired objects) in his immediate environment, and to use foresight to solve simple problems. Based on observed correlations, Bates et al. (1979) have concluded that early tool use (use of strings, pillows and sticks to obtain objects) draws on a cognitive structure similar to that underlying the use of persons to obtain desired objects. Other researchers (Synder, 1978; Zachry, 1978) have reported a strong relationship between foresightful problemsolving and more symbolic use of language (e.g., reference to perceptually absent objects, nonperceptual characteristics of objects, such as ownership and word combinations).

We have adapted The Development of Operational Causality Scale (Seibert & Hogan, 1979) to exclude items that are social in nature (e.g., when the spectacle is a person or when the way to have a spectacle repeated is through another person). For this reason, the imitation scales have been excluded from this discussion as well. The Causality scale describes the child's developing strategies for re-activating objects that create interesting sights and sounds. Most research conducted to explore the relationship of this scale to communication measures has focused on the social aspects of causal agency (e.g,, Harding & Golinkoff, 1979) and so is not relevant to this discussion.

The Construction of Object Relations in Space assesses the child's ability to use and understand spatial concepts related to reverse side, on top of, upside down, detours and the role of gravity. While this scale has been found to show little relationship to communication and language (e.g., Bates et al., 1979; Zachry, 1978), it has been suggested by Brown (1973) and Edwards (1973) that such sensori-motor spatial concepts precede the appearance of relational terms or locatives such as "in," "on," and "under".

The Development of Schemes for Relating to Objects assesses the child's increasingly complex and discriminative actions on objects, culminating in recognition of their functional or socially appropriate use. Symbolic or pretend play has been viewed as an upward extension of the skills represented in this scale by a number of investigators (e.g., Fenson, Kagan, Kearsley & Zelazo, 1976; Nicolich, 1977; Seibert & Hogan, 1979). Socially appropriate use of objects has been hypothesized to be an index of the presence of the conceptual basis for object reference (e.g., Bates, Bretherton, Shore & Carpen, 1979; Nelson, 1974; Seibert, 1979) and data support this link (Hogan, Seibert & Mundy, 1980). The playful and combinatorial skills involved in certain symbolic play developments have been hypothesized by Nicolich (in press) to parallel the structure of the skills involved in early word combinations.

In addition to these specific relationships, it has sometimes been argued that a certain level of sensorimotor development (typically related to stage 5 or stage 6 of Piaget's sensorimotor stages) is necessary for certain communicative and linguistic developments. According to the general framework and supporting data (e.g., Ingram, 1978; Miller, Chapman, Branston & Riechle, 1980), such an hypothesis is correct if all that is meant is that certain communicative or linguistic developments co-occur with or are manifestations of stage 5 or stage 6 sensorimoter organization. But the more specific claim, that sensorimotor skills with objects reflecting these stages of development are prerequisites to certain social-communicative developments, is almost certainly wrong. There are enough exceptions to suggest that observed sequences in order of acquisition between object and social skills are only typical and not invariant sequences. There may be a number of explanations, related to opportunities for appropriate experiences and different information processing demands, that could account for the typical sequences without concluding that the object skills are prerequisite to the social-linguistic skills. Any search for prerequisites requires careful analysis of skills at both a behavioral and conceptual level to determine what skills and concepts are components of other skills.

We would, however, agree that there is a more general sense in which object cognitive skills are necessary for communication skills. Skills with objects provide a foundation of knowledge of the physical world about which the child may communicate to a partner. Without knowledge of or interest in the object world, the child will have little reason to communicate with another except to engage in pure social interaction. Knowledge about objects is at the center of most communicative exchanges.

An analysis of the social domain. In the same manner that Piaget took the concepts and skills of the competent two-year old as a reference point in describing development, the proposed model adopts a similar perspective in analyzing the social domain. The communicative skills of the two-year old, on the verge of symbolic communication skills, provide the reference point in proposing developmental dimensions for the social domain. Our analysis of this domain is based on a review of recent literature in developmental psycholinguistics, mother-infant interaction, attachment and early social cognitive development. The set of developmental dimensions is intended to incorporate most behaviors typically considered in the area of infant social and communication development, organized from the model's pragmatic orientation. As with any system of categorization, some distinctions are made at the expense of others, reflecting our own biases and priorities about what is important in early communication development. Distinctions have been included that the competent practitioner may make, but that are not explicitly represented in available instruments for assessing social and communicative development.

Table 1 represents the categories used to analyze the social domain into component dimensions. The three column headings represent three broad pragmatic functions that can be identified in early interactions before language emerges.

Table 1
Generating the Social-Communications Dimensions

	Functions		
ROLES	SOCIAL INTERACTION	JOINT ATTENTION	BEHAVIOR REGULATION
Responding	RSI	RJA	RBR
Initiating	ISI	IJA	IBA
Maintaining	MSI	MJA	

Social Interaction encompasses behaviors that have as their primary goal and function the establishment of attention to self, with no objective except playful interaction between self and other. The quality of these interactions typically is nondirective and nondemanding, except insofar as one partner is demanding attention to and acknowledgement of self from the other. This dimension overlaps with several previously identified early communicative functions including Halliday's (1975) interactive and imaginative functions, Dore's (1975) speech act categories of calling and greeting, and Bruner's (1975b) social exchange routines.

Joint Attention refers to interactions in which one partner is attempting to direct the other's attention to an object, person or event for the primary purpose of sharing attention, that is, of looking at the same thing together. At the higher levels, joint attention activities lead into linguistic communicative functions focused on information exchange, or shared attention about details of entities,

events, and situations. Bruner (1975a, 1975b) has emphasized this dimension for its importance to language development. This dimension overlaps with Bates et al.'s (1975)
protodeclarative, Halliday's (1975) informative and heuristic functions, and Dore's (1975) speech act categories of
labeling, answering and requesting answer.

Behavior Regulation includes behaviors for which one
partner is attempting to direct or regulate the other's
behavior, typically to achieve an external goal. Often,
behavior regulation occurs in the form of enlisting the
assistance of another in order to have a need met. The
goal of the interaction may also be either to restrict the
activity or to elicit a compliant action from the partner.
This dimension overlaps with Bates et al.'s (1975) proto-
imperative, Halliday's (1975) instrumental and regulatory
functions, and Dore's (1975) speech act categories of requesting action and protesting.

Although skills related to all three dimensions are
developing concurrently, the following somewhat oversimpli-
fied analysis of their relationship to each other in the
child's development of intentional communication skills may
be of heuristic value. The child must first become skillful
in non-goal-oriented interaction with social partners,
learning that their attention is worth gaining and maintaining (the focus of the Social Interaction dimension). As
the child appreciates the reciprocal interactive possibilities with a social partner, the attention of the dyad can be
expanded to encompass a third entity or event (the focus of
the Joint Attention dimension). With an appreciation that
he can simultaneously have the partner's attention on himself and on an object, the child can purposefully use shared
attention to gain the partner's assistance in achieving
goals such as obtaining objects out of reach (an important
aspect of the Behavior Regulation dimension). The logical
progression expands from control of skills related to attention to self, to control of skills related to attention both
to self and to object, to control of skills related to
attention both to self and to object in order to achieve a
goal with the object.

The three rows in Table 1 represent role aspects of
communicative interaction that cut across the three functions just described. Common objects in the child's envi-

ronment do not initiate interaction but only react to the
child's or other's actions on them.   In contrast, persons
are interactive and either partner may be in the role of
initiator or responder.   These complementary roles are
represented in the first two rows.   In addition, for the
Social Interaction and Joint Attention functions, the child
should be able to participate in interaction sequences in a
dialogue-like manner.   In other words, the child must become
skillful at maintaining these interactions.   This aspect is
represented as a separate role in the third row.   Table 1
presents the role-by-function categories resulting from the
intersection of the columns and the rows.   Each acronym
represents a communicative dimension in the model's classification system, each of which has provided the conceptual
basis for an individual assessment scale.   Each scale is
comprised of behavioral items sequenced developmentally in
approximate order of acquisition.   The source of these items
includes others' descriptions of early social and communicative behaviors and transcripts of videotaped observations of
social-communicative interactions with over eighty high-risk
and handicapped infants and toddlers.

The traditional receptive-expressive distinction represented in many communication scales is not explicitly included within the model's classification system with its
pragmatic orientation.   Distinguishing between receptive and
expressive skills represents an input-output distinction,
based on an information-processing orientation.   Receptive
and expressive skills are included in the scales.   However,
the pragmatic distinction between responding and initiating
does not lead to the same organization of skills that the
receptive-expressive distinction produces.

Our primary goal has been to delineate functions that
can be accomplished without language, but that continue to
be represented in the child's single-word productions and
early word combinations.   Consistent with a pragmatic orientation, the model has focused on functions rather than
linguistic form and content.   Once the child is becoming a
linguistic communicator, the practitioner should supplement
the information derived from this categorization system with
analyses of semantic relations and syntactic complexity
(e.g., see Bloom & Lahey, 1978; Miller, 1981).   Semantic and
syntactic analyses should not replace a pragmatic analysis,
however, simply because the child has language.   Communica-

tive functions served by speech are as important an area for
assessment as those functions served by prelinguistic gestures.

Cognitive level analysis. This section provides a
horizontal analysis of the cognitive domain, according to
the levels suggested by the cognitive developmental theory.
The characterization of early cognitive development as a
series of hierarchical levels of organization is not new;
Piaget (1952, 1954) offered such a description of development years ago. However, only recently have investigators
(e.g., McCall, Eichorn, & Hogarty, 1977; Uzgiris, 1976,
1977; Wachs & Hubert, 1980) provided empirical support for
such a series of stages to characterize the early development of knowledge and problem-solving skills with persons
and with objects. The proposed model uses the terminology
and distinctions introduced by Uzgiris (1976, 1977) to
characterize the successive levels of cognitive organization. Ideas have been borrowed from Bates et al. (1979),
Fischer (1980), McCall et al. (1977), and Sugerman-Bell
(1978) as well.

Level 0 (approximately birth to two months) may be
described as primarily responsive or reflexive. The infant's actions are usually elicited by the changing physical
and social stimulation around him.

Level 1 (approximately two to seven months) is characterized by simple, undifferentiated actions. It marks the
beginning of voluntary activity by the infant. Although
capable of making visual and auditory discriminations, the
infant at this level does not coordinate them systematically
with his actions toward persons and objects. His actions on
objects are simple and repetitive. His social interactions
imply recognition of people (e.g., social smile) but there
is little evidence that he actively differentiates among
persons.

Level 2 (approximately eight to twelve months) corre-
sponds to the development of complex, differentiated
actions. There are indications at this level that the
child's perceptual discriminations among objects and people
in his environment are being coordinated with his actions
toward them. But actions toward objects and actions toward
people are not coordinated with each other. Desires and

goals related to objects become evident in the child's behavior, but the social partner, while perceived as a source of social interaction, is not yet understood as a means to achieving object goals.

Level 3 (approximately 13-18 mos.) is characterized by regulation of one's own behavior using differentiated feedback. It is not until this level is reached that there is a flexibility in the infant's actions that allows him to alter his behavior in subtle ways to achieve success in problem-solving situations. Solutions are discovered through deliberate trial-and-error. The child begins to demonstrate an understanding both of what does and what does not work in simple problem situations. This level is characterized also by the beginning conventionalization of signals and the ability to coordinate attention simultaneously to both objects and people. People are used to solve "object-problems" (e.g., getting an object) and objects are used to solve "people-problems" (e.g., giving an object in order to get another's attention to oneself). Level 3 initiating skills usually require the coordination of a gesture or action on an object with eye contact to the adult. According to the proposed model once a child is using single words in addition to or as a substitute for gestures, social-communication skills are classified at sub-level 3.5. The earliest conventionalizations of sounds as words does not require a symbolic level of cognitive organization, because the objects are perceptually present and context still helps carry the word's meaning. Consequently, the transition from words is marked only by a sub-level distinction.

At level 4 (approximately 19 to 24 months) which is characterized by anticipatory regulation, the child's problem-solving becomes symbolic as he becomes capable of mental action or thought. Trial-and-error is at times replaced by insightful solutions to problems. Symbolic or representational abilities are hypothesized to provide the foundation for a number of developments related to language, pretend play and delayed observational learning. Communication begins to occur solely through linguistic means at this level, as some words begin to be combined generatively, indexing their status as symbols rather than perceptually bound signals. This overview only touches on the range of developments that characterize each cognitive level. The interested reader is referred to Fischer (1980), McCall

(McCall et al., 1977; McCall, 1979), and Uzgiris (1976, 1977) for their discussions of the levels.

Synthesis of the dimensions and the levels. Each scale dimension or task sequence as noted earlier, can be characterized as passing through a similar sequence of development, based on the levels of increasing cognitive complexity just described. Tasks from different dimensions can therefore be equated at a structural level in terms of the general cognitive organization they require for mastery. For example, there should be at least one task for each social scale involving complex, differentiated action patterns that measures the child's Level 2 skills. The model asserts that all such level 2 tasks across all scales index a similar level of cognitive complexity and should be mastered at approximately the same point in development, given equal opportunity for experience for each task.

Table 2 shows the organizational matrix that results when all of the vertical developmental dimensions are laid over the horizontal levels. We are in the process of developing an assessment instrument for the social domain, called the Early Social-Communication Scales (ESCS). The instrument is comprised of items derived by selecting at least one task or skill from each social dimension, representative of each developmental level, for each box in the matrix. Examples of how this process has been applied to a scale from each domain are presented in Table 3.1

This synthesis enables one to construct an overall integrated picture of the child's relative levels of functioning across all of the object and social dimensions. A child's pattern of strengths and weaknesses, accelerated and lagging areas, across all the dimensions, relative to the cognitive organizational level, should become readily apparent. Each item does not simply represent an isolated object or social skill, but can be considered in the context of its relationship both to the developmental dimension that it is a part of and to the child's overall functioning across all cognitive scale dimensions in both domains. The horizontal and vertical lines in the matrix, because of the conceptual organization they impose, are the critical elements of the assessment instrument rather than the specific item pool. Individual items lose much of their significance if their relationship to the horizontal and vertical dimen-

Table 2

Organizational Matrix for Object and Social Dimensions by Levels

	Object Dimensions					Social Dimensions							
	Visual pursuit and Object Permanence	Means for Obtaining Desired Events	Operational Causality	Object Relations in Space	Schemes for Relating to Objects*	Responding to Social Interaction	Initiating Social Interaction	Maintaining Social Interaction	Responding to Joint Attention	Initiating Joint Attention	Maintaining Joint Attention	Responding to Behavior Regulation*	Initiating Behavior Regulation
Level 0 Responsive													
Level 1 Simple Voluntary Undifferentiated													
Level 2 Complex Differentiated													
Level 3 Regulation by Feedback													
Level 4 Anticipatory Regulation													

*See Table 3 for Examples of Scale Item Content Organized by Levels.

sions is eliminated or ignored. In fact, other assessment instruments contain many similar items. A generative application of the model would be to observe a specific behavior and locate its position in the matrix by judging the behavior's object or social function and its level of complexity.

It is this synthesis of dimensions with levels that is intended to simplify the array of categories generated by the horizontal and vertical analyses. Categories are organized into one comprehensive framework that should make the model's application feasible for the practitioner.

Empirical Support for the Model

The proposed model is intended to organize a broad array of early social and object skills into a single system; however, psychological reality of the model must be verified. Ultimately, the model's usefulness depends on its validity. Our research objective has been to test the model's central hypothesis of shared levels of cognitive organization underlying the object and social domains. Specifically, the model predicts that, if equal opportunity is provided for experiences with both object and social skills, on the average, a child's level of performance should be the same across domains. Within a large representative sample of children, therefore, most children should have nearly equal scores for both domains, if items have been appropriately equated for level of complexity. Individual exceptions to this congruence may occur as a result of intra-individual differences both in motivation and in opportunities for experience between the two domains. In such cases, a child will show higher performance in one domain compared to the other. Within the entire sample, however, the pattern of discrepancies should be equally distributed on either side of the zero difference point. In addition, large discrepancies between the two domains are predicted to be less likely to occur than smaller discrepancies. Therefore, the total distribution of difference scores for the entire sample should approximate a normal distribution, with a mode at zero.

The data to evaluate the predicted congruence between domains were gathered by administering our adapted version of the Uzgiris-Hunt scales (modified to have an almost

Table 3

Examples of Scales from the Object Domain and the Social-Communication Domain, Organized According to the Five Structural Levels

	Object Domain: Schemes for Relating to Objects	Social-Communication Domain: Responding to Another's Attempt at Behavior Regulation (RBR)
0 (0-2 mos.) Responsive	Holds or grasps object placed in hand	Can be soothed
1 (2-7 mos.) Simple Voluntary Undifferentiated	Uses only simple action patterns on all objects (e.g., mouthing, banging, waving)	a. Turns to other's voice b. Resists releasing object pulled by other
2 (8-13 mos.) Complex Differentiated	Uses different actions for different objects (e.g., stretches elastic, rubs cotton)	a. inhibits action to "No" or other sharp vocalization b. looks to other and protests as other takes object away
3 (13-18 mos.) Regulation by Feedback	Uses objects in socially influenced ways (e.g., combs hair, wears necklace) --- As objects are presented, spontaneously names them without looking to other	Comprehends at least two simple commands accompanied by gestures --- Comprehends at least two simple commands in context, without accompanying gestures
4 (18 mos. +) Anticipatory Regulation	Use objects in symbolic play (e.g., pretends block is car, or banana is telephone)	Follows a series of simple contrastive commands presented without accompanying gestures and with minimal context

exclusive focus on object skills) and the Early Social Communication Scales (ESCS) to 81 high risk and handicapped
infants and toddlers (4 mos. to 3 yrs. 6 mos.) enrolled in a
program of early intervention during the past two years. It
was assumed that the intervention program, in general,
provided equal opportunity for experiences relevant to both
domains. The total sample included 23 high risk, 15 Down's
Syndrome, 8 cerebral-palsied, 8 emotionally disturbed, 4
hearing impaired, 1 visually impaired, and 22 other children
with varying degrees of retardation (mild to severe) of
various or unknown etiologies. Our use of such a heterogeneous sample was intentional and its purpose will be noted
later. Each child received a level score (from 0 to 4) for
each scale, which represented the highest level at which he
passed an item in that scale. A mean object level score and
a mean social level score were computed for each child by
calculating the average of his individual scale scores for
each domain. The difference between the mean level of
performance for the two domains constituted the datum of
interest. Specifically, each child's mean object level
score was subtracted from his mean socio-communication
score. Since some children have been tested more than once
(at 3 or 6 month intervals); a total of 121 difference
scores was available for analysis.

Figure 1 presents the frequency histogram for mean
level difference scores between the object and social
domains, in .4 level intervals, for all 121 test administra-
tions. The zero point was defined as -.2 to +.2, to allow
for measurement error. While the distribution is somewhat
negatively skewed (suggesting a tendency for object scores
to lead social scores), there is a very definite mode at
zero, with roughly equal numbers of children falling on
either side of this zero point, in decreasing frequency for
greater differences.

One may question whether the congruence observed between the object and social scores reflects a specifically
cognitive organization underlying the domains or instead is
a manifestation of a more general function that underlies
all aspects of development, regardless of presumed cognitive
capacities. For example, across a two-year developmental
span, measures such as height, weight, chronological age and
psychomotor age may be expected to correlate almost as
highly with the measures gathered. Because this issue has

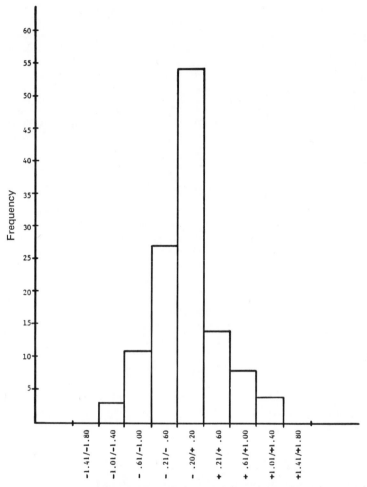

Differences in Overall Mean Communication Level Relative to Overall Mean
Object Cognition Level in .4 Stage Intervals

Figure 1. Distribution of discrepancies between mean social-communication level and
mean object level for 121 data points.

been addressed in another paper (Seibert, 1980), only a summary of the results is offered here. Basically, the strategy was to constitute certain subsamples from the total heterogeneous sample, first by eliminating children who were not handicapped but only at risk, and then by including only children above thirty months of age chronologically or children whose mental age and psychomotor age, as measured by the Bayley Scales, were different from each other by four months or more. Regardless of how the subsamples were constituted, the correlation between the ESCS and the Uzgiris-Hunt scores remained high and virtually unchanged (equal to approximately r=85). Yet the relationship of these measures to both chronological age (a measure of opportunity for experience) and psychomotor age (a measure of motor development) was reduced and even eliminated in the specially constructed subsamples.

Additional support for the cognitive base of the observed relationship comes from a study by Mundy, Seibert, Hogan & Fagan (1981). Reliable correlations were found between the object and social measures and a measure of infant visual recognition memory. The recognition measure minimizes the need for motor skills in assessing an aspect of basic cognitive functioning; the child need only have intact vision to indicate his preference on the tasks. This cognitive measure also showed little relationship to level of motor development or chronological age in a subset of the handicapped sample studied.

Further research must be conducted to establish the model's validity. Nevertheless, the model provides a comprehensive system, with empirical support, that can guide the practitioner in making decisions about early intervention in prelinguistic communication development.

Assessment and Intervention Implications

This final section addresses implications of the model for assessment and intervention. For purposes of discussion, assessment has been broken down into a Gathering Information phase and a Summarizing and Interpreting phase. Intervention has been broken down into a Planning phase and an Implementing phase. The emphasis and source of examples for the discussion is primarily the social-communication domain.

Assessment Gathering Information. One of the goals of
the model is to expand and refine the practitioner's observational categories by suggesting what behaviors are worthy
of note and why. Comprehensive assessment requires both a
decision-making process to make judgments about what is
being observed and means to assure that such behaviors occur
at a frequent enough rate to be observed reliably.

The model suggests a series of decisions that the
practitioner must make in judging each of a child's cognitive behaviors. The first decision is whether the observed
behavior more appropriately belongs to the object or the
social domain. Next, it must be decided to which scale
dimension the behavior most appropriately belongs. In the
object domain, the adult-imposed structure of the testing
situation typically determines within which scale the
child's behavior is scored. In the social domain, because
the child can spontaneously initiate interaction as well as
respond to the adult-imposed structure, this is true to a
lesser degree. In the social domain, the decision about
dimensions has two parts: 1) what pragmatic function does
the behavior primarily serve (i.e., Social Interaction,
Joint Attention or Behavior Regulation) and 2) is the child
initiating or responding and is he maintaining the interaction. Following this decision, the practitioner must judge
what developmental level the behavior represents. Moving
through this series of decisions allows the practitioner to
place individual behaviors within a single box in the matrix. Finally, the practitioner must decide whether adequate opportunities for behaviors at levels higher than that
at which the child is performing are being provided. If
not, such opportunities should be made available in an
attempt to observe and elicit optimal performance. Although
the assessment scales (ESCS) developed from the model provide at least one specific behavioral eliciting situation
for each box in the matrix, an ideal, generative application
of the model should allow the practitioner to move through
the decision-making process to classify nearly any behavior
observed from a developmentally young child within the
matrix.

One of the advantages of this approach for work with
multiply handicapped children is that it suggests a meaningful framework for evaluating their behaviors when they are
incapable of responding within traditional, standardized

testing situations. Such an application of the model obviously is not simply a routine matter, but requires a full understanding of the model, that is, of the significance of the horizontal and vertical lines in the matrix and not merely the individual item content.

In considering effective means for eliciting social-communicative behaviors, the practitioner should first be aware that certain materials and situations increase the probability of observing both initiating and responding behaviors on the part of the child. For example, games involving physical interaction and objects that are commonly used in social routines may increase the probability of observing behaviors related to Social Interaction. Pictures on the wall and picture books set the stage for Joint Attention activities. Desirable toys that are visible to the child, but out of reach, or that create interesting spectacles, but are difficult to activate can lead to the observation of skills related to Behavior Regulation.

A decision also needs to be made about who will be interacting with the child for the assessment. For a number of reasons, the child's own caregiver may appear to be the preferred partner. However, exclusive reliance on observations of caregiver-child interactions may fail to generate enough information to fill out the matrix for every scale dimension.2 Consequently, the practitioner may need to join the interaction rather than continue to observe at a distance. Certain additional responsibilities for the practitioner accompany this more active role, because the quality and direction of that interaction is influenced in important ways by both partners. A balance of parent report, observations of caregiver-child interaction, and semi-structured interactions between the practitioner and the child may yield the most useful information.

With appropriate materials and a good sense of how to participate in the process, the practitioner should be able to gather information on the child's optimal level of performance in each scale. Failure to observe behaviors at earlier levels in a scale becomes less important when the child demonstrates skills at a higher level.

Assessment: Summarizing and Interpreting. If the information-gathering phase is thorough, a judgment about a child's level of performance in each scale dimension should be possible. Profiles can be used to summarize the results for both the object scales and the social-communication scales. The highest level in each scale at which a child is credited with a behavior represents the child's score for that scale. The completed profile provides a picture of the child's relative level of performance across the different domains and dimensions. The individual scale scores then can be organized in various ways. Mean level is the average of the scores for all the dimensions. Optimal level is the highest level observed for the child in any of the scales; modal level is the most frequent level observed (Fischer, 1980). If optimal and modal level are nearly the same, the child is probably functioning close to his potential. If optimal level is higher than modal level, the child may have potential that can be developed with opportunities for relevant experience.

If the child displays a peak performance in one or a small number of scales that is discrepant from his modal level, the practitioner should conduct additional assessment probes to determine if that performance is reliable behavior or merely a chance or very infrequent occurrence. If the peak performance is reliable, the practitioner should ask whether the lower performance on other scales represents legitimate failure by the child. Although the structural level assumption of the model leads to the development of expectations about what skills a child should have, the practitioner should attempt to maintain objectivity. In particular, it is important to guard against misinterpeting or ignoring behaviors because they do not fit the practitioner's developing set about a child. In fact, uneven profiles with skills at different levels across different dimensions have been more the rule than the exception in the samples of children we have assessed. In addition, different children with the same overall mean level scores may exhibit dramatically different profile patterns. Data from the profiles can also be used to compare subsets of scales. The child's mean level of performance with objects, found by computing the average of the object scale scores, can be compared to his mean level of social-communication performance (summarized for the entire sample in Figure 1). The child's mean levels of performance for the different pragmatic functions also can be compared, as well as his mean levels of initiating and responding skills.

The goal of the information gathering, summarizing and interpreting is, of course, to make decisions about actual intervention. The next section considers how the model and the kinds of assessment information just described can guide the practitioner in this process.

Intervention: Planning. One of the primary functions of assessment is to aid the practitioner in establishing objectives for intervention. The model provides a basis for establishing intervention objectives that are broader than typical behavioral objectives. Although concern for accountability in education has had the healthy effect of focusing the practitioner on specifically defined behavioral objectives, a balance needs to be struck between specificity and generality. Functions and concepts are more appropriately the objectives of intervention in the cognitive domains than are specific behaviors (Seibert, in press). Objectives should be defined in terms of a range or class of behaviors that accomplish a similar function (e.g., how to enlist another's assistance in obtaining desired objects) or that represent a similar concept (e.g., objects have names) rather than as specific behaviors. The implicit but untested assumption is that establishing more broadly defined objectives may help reduce the need for generalization training because, from the outset, the child is learning and applying a range of behaviors in a variety of situations.

At a more general level, the model suggests that the goal of intervention in the cognitive domains is to facilitate the child's development of higher levels of functioning across all of the scale dimensions. The analysis of the domains into multiple scales should help the practitioner distribute attention across the dimensions. In practical terms, the model should prompt the realization that the child should be developing initiating as well as responding skills across all dimensions. Often, behavioral objectives for language are written only in terms of responding under adult stimulus control, that is, with a Behavior Regulation focus. The other functions and roles are often overlooked.

The completed profiles for a child should alert the practitioner to the child's strengths and weaknesses, indicating which dimensions are underdeveloped and in greater need of facilitation. An hypothesis derived from the model is that the lagging areas may respond most quickly to intervention. The rationale for this prediction is that more advanced development in other scales (optimal levels) indexes the presence of underlying cognitive organization needed to acquire deficient skills in lagging dimensions. The child may simply require opportunities for appropriate experiences in the deficient areas. In comparison, facilitating the development of skills at levels higher than the child's current optimal level may be more difficult because the child is not yet manifesting any behaviors indicative of the higher levels of cognitive organization. What experiences are appropriate may not be so easily determined. Different intervention strategies may be required for the two situations (Seibert, in press). While it may appear that developmental ages from norm-referenced assessments can provide the same information about patterns of strengths and weaknesses that is generated by an analysis of the levels, there is an important difference. Developmental age estimates are empirical norms based on the chronological ages at which skills are typically acquired in natural environments. Structural level estimates provide a meaningful basis, grounded in a theory of cognitive organization, for analyzing skills, examining relationships among the dimensions and judging when skills may be attainable, dependent on chronological age.

Intervention: Implementing. The model's descriptions of the organization of the child's cognitive structures at the different levels provides a basis for determining what kinds of interactions and general classes of experiences are most important at each level (Uzgiris, 1977). Knowledge of what the social and physical environments look like from the child's perspective suggests what experiences may either reinforce and expand that perspective or challenge it. The model has relevance for making decisions about appropriate materials, arrangement of the physical environment, the nature and focus of adult-child interactions, staff-child ratios, the role of peers and the use of schedules and routines as a function of the child's developmental level. Efforts are beginning to be directed at articulating these implications (de la Vega, 1981).

The focus of intervention in the social-communication domain is on interaction. The nature and quality of that interaction depends on both partners. To achieve the balanced set of objectives that foster development across all

of the dimensions, the practitioner must be sensitive to a
number of issues that bear on the nature of their interaction. Are all interactions recognized for their potential
to foster social and communication skills? In addition to
making demands on the child, is the practitioner ready to
respond to the child's initiations? If the child is hesi-
tant to initiate, are strategies available for arranging the
physical environment to encourage the child's initiation?
In addition, does the practitioner know how to hold back and
wait for the child's initiations? Does the practitioner
know how the child can be helped to maintain a turn-taking
sequence for a series of turns? What is reasonable to
expect of the child, given his developmental level? When is
it appropriate to increase the demands for higher level
skills? Are opportunities for less-structured playful
Social Interaction and Joint Attention activities provided
in a reasonable balance with the more didactic interaction
style reflected in the Behavior Regulation dimension? This
balance is important, but perhaps difficult to achieve
because teaching is so often equated with adult-directed
activity. Does the practitioner realize that it is not
simply the materials and the topography of the behaviors
that determine the nature of the interaction? Communicative
functions reflect each partner's intent. Even a common
social game can be turned from Social Interaction to Behavior Regulation if the adult becomes intent on demanding
only one type of response. Social Interaction allows the
child some freedom in selecting among responses. Once a
specific behavior is being demanded of the child, the interaction moves into the category of Behavior Regulaton. The
appeal of arranging most "training" interactions so that the
child is responding to the practitioner's direction may be
that it is possible to define from the outset where the
interaction is going and what the outcome should be, in
terms of a trained behavior under stimulus control. If the
practitioner has few categories for analyzing and interpreting the child's other interactions, and especially the
child's initiations, the fear is that the child may take the
interaction in an unknown direction that may not be productive. However, within the model, categories exist for
defining most of the child's initiations as well as his
responses. As a result, more flexibility can be introduced
into the interaction, because the practitioner can anticipate where the interaction is going and influence its direction, without becoming over-regulating. It is not that

limits on a child's behavior should not be set or that
demands should never be made. A child who repeatedly refuses to accept direction from others becomes a less desirable partner and, as a result, may lose out on valuable
opportunities for important communication experiences. The
goal is a balance among all the dimensions. With an awareness of how the partner affects the nature and quality of
the child's interactions, the practitioner should be in a
position to achieve that balance.

Summary

In this paper, a model for analyzing and relating the
development of early social and object skills has been
described. The model has implications for a number of
intervention decisions that the practitioner must make.
However, to apply the model in a practical context requires
more details than it is possible to provide in a single
chapter. The goal of the paper has been to make the practitioner aware of an alternative approach to early social-communication development leading to language. The model is
dynamic, not static, and still in a state of evolution. The
practitioner interested in applying the model must be willing to be thoughtful and creative, because the model is
complex, and because the processes to be facilitated are
complex. What the model suggests is an integrated way of
looking at very young children's social and object skills
that says something about how we should interact with them.
Determining whether the perspective is valid will require
additional research, and evaluating its practicality will
require additional efforts at application. However, we
believe the potential benefits make finding out worth the
effort.

NOTES

[1] The complete set of scales for the social domain is
still in draft form, having undergone several revisions.
The most recent draft of the profile is available from the
authors.

[2] For example, some behaviors in the ESCS vary in their
level value depending on whether the child uses eye contact
in coordination with the behavior. If the caregiver talks
throughout the interaction, the observer may not be able to

determine whether any of the child's eye contact with/to the caregiver has been spontaneous or has been elicited by the caregiver's talking.

REFERENCES

Bates, E., Benigni, L., Bretherton, I., Camaioni, L., & Volterra, V. The emergence of symbols: Cognition and communication in infancy. New York: Academic Press, 1979.

Bates, E., Bretherton, I., Shore, C., & Carpen, K. The emergence of symbols in language and action: The role of contextual support. Paper presented at the meeting of the Society for Research in Child Development, San Francisco, March 1979.

Bates, E., Camaioni, L., & Volterra, V. The acquisition of performatives prior to speech. Merrill-Palmer Quarterly, 1975, 21, 205-226.

Bloom, L. One word at a time. The Hague: Mouton, 1973.

Bloom, L., & Lahey, M. Language development and language disorders. New York: Wiley, 1978.

Brown, R. A first language: The early stages. Cambridge, MA: Harvard University Press, 1973.

Bruner, J.S. From communication to language - A psychological perspective. Cognition, 1975a 3, 255-287.

Bruner, J.S. The ontogenesis of speech acts. Journal of Child Language, 1975b, 2, 1-19.

Bullowa, M. (Ed.). Before speech: The beginning of interpersonal communication. Cambridge: Cambridge University Press, 1979.

Corrigan, R. Patterns of individual communication and cognitive development. Unpublished doctoral dissertation, University of Denver, 1976.

Corrigan, R. Language development as related to stage 6 object permanence development. Journal of Child Language, 1977, 5, 173-189.

de la Vega, M. Curriculum implications of the ESCS. Unpublished material, University of Miami, Mailman Center for Child Development, 1981.

Dore, J. Holophrases, speech acts and language universals. Journal of Child Language, 1975, 2, 21-40.

Edwards, D. Sensorimotor intelligence and semantic relations in early child grammar. Cognition, 1973, 2, 395-434.

Fenson, L., Kagan, J., Kearsley, R.B., & Zelazo, P.R. The developmental progression of manipulative play in the first two years. Child Development, 1976, 47, 232-236.

Fischer, K.W. A theory of cognitive development: The control and construction of hierarchies of skills. Psychological Review, 1980, 87, 477-531.

Fischer, K.W., & Corrigan, R. A skill approach to language development. In R. Stark (Ed.), Language behavior in infancy and early childhood. Amsterdam: Elsevier-North Holland, in press.

Halliday, M.A.K. Learning how to mean. In E.H. Lenneberg & E. Lenneberg (Eds.), Foundations of language development, Vol. 1. New York: Academic Press, 1975.

Harding, C.G., & Golinkoff, R.M. The origins of intentional vocalizations in prelinguistic infants. Child Development, 1979, 50, 33-40.

Hogan, A.E., Seibert, J.M., & Mundy, P.C. The emergence of object labels in developmentally delayed toddlers: Implications for intervention and for a theory of early reference. Paper presented at the Fifth Annual Boston University Conference on Language Development, Boston, October 1980.

Hubley, P., & Trevarthen, C. Sharing a task in infancy. In I.C. Uzgiris (Ed.), Social interaction and communication during infancy. San Francisco: Josey-Bass, 1979.

Ingram, D. Sensorimotor intelligence and language development. In A. Lock (Ed.), Action, gesture and symbol: The emergence of language. New York: Academic Press, 1979.

McCall, R.B. Qualitative transitions in behavioral develop-
    ment in the first two years of life. In M.H. Bornstein
    & W. Kessen (Eds.), Psychological development from in-
    fancy: Image to intention. Hillsdale, NJ: Lawrence
    Erlbaum, 1979.

McCall, R., Eichorn, D., & Hogarty, P. Transitions in early
    mental development. Monographs of the Society for Re-
    search in Child Development, 1977, 42 (3), No. 171.

Miller, J.F. Assessing children's language behavior: A
    developmental process approach. In R.L. Schiefelbusch
    (Ed.), Bases of language intervention. Baltimore:
    University Park Press, 1978.

Miller, J.F., Chapman, R.S., Branston, M.B., & Reichle, J.
    Language comprehension in sensorimotor stage V and VI.
    Journal of Speech and Hearing Research, 1980, 23,
    284-311.

Morehead, D., & Morehead, A. From signal to sign: A Pia-
    getian view of thought and language during the first
    two years. In R.L. Schiefelbusch & L.L. Lloyd (Eds.),
    Language perspectives, acquisition, retardation, and
    intervention. Baltimore: University Park Press, 1974.

Mundy, P.C., Seibert, J.M., Hogan, A.E., & Fagan, J. Recog-
    nition memory in handicapped infants. Paper presented
    at the Fourteenth Annual Gatlinburg Conference on
    Research in MR/DD, Gatlinburg, March 1981.

Nelson, K. Concept, word and sentence: Interrelations in
    acquisition and development. Psychological Review,
    1974, 81, 276-285.

Nicolich, L. McCune. Beyond sensorimotor intelligence:
    Assessment of symbolic maturity through analysis of
    pretend play. Merrill Palmer Quarterly, 1977, 23,
    89-99.

Nicolich, L. McCune. Toward symbolic functioning: Struc-
    ture of early pretend games and potential parallels
    with language. Child Development, in press.

Piaget, J. The origins of intelligence in children. New
    York: International Universities Press, 1952.

Piaget, J. The construction of reality in the child. New
    York: Basic Books, 1954.

Rees, N.S. Pragmatics of language: Applications to normal
    and disordered language development. In R.L. Schiefel-
    busch (Ed.), Bases of language intervention. Balti-
    more: University Park Press, 1978.

Seibert, J.M.   A model for analyzing the development of
    early communication skills, based on levels of cogni-
    tive organization. Paper presented at the Fourth
    Annual Boston University Conference on Language Devel-
    opment, Boston, September 1979.

Seibert, J.M. Developmental assessment based on a struc-
    tural stage model of early communication development:
    Some theoretical, methodological and practical issues.
    Paper presented at the Thirteenth Annual Gatlinburg
    Conference on Research in Mental Retardation and Devel-
    opmental Disabilities, Gatlinburg, Tennessee, March
    1980.

Seibert, J.M. Use of the scales of psychological develop-
    ment in early intervention programs. To be published
    in I.C. Uzgiris & J.McV. Hunt (Eds.), Research with
    scales of psychological development in infancy.
    Urbana, IL: University of Illinois Press, in press.

Seibert, J.M., & Hogan, A.E. Debbie School Sensorimotor
    Performance Profile (adapted from Uzgiris and Hunt,
    1975). Unpublished material, University of Miami,
    Mailman Center for Child Development, 1979.

Seibert, J.M., & Oller, D.K. Linguisitc pragmatics and
    language intervention strategies. Journal of Autism
    and Developmental Disorders, in press.

Snyder, L. Communicative and cognitive abilities and dis-
    abilities in the sensorimotor period. Merrill -
    Palmer Quarterly, 1978, 24 (3), 161-180.

Sugarman-Bell, S. Some organizational aspects of pre-verbal
    communication. In I. Markova (Ed.), The social context
    of language. New York: Wiley & Sons, 1978.

Uzgiris, I.C. Organization of sensorimotor intelligence.
    In M. Lewis (Ed.), Origins of intelligence. New York:
    Plenum, 1976.

Uzgiris, I.C. Plasticity and structure. In I.C. Uzgiris &
    F. Weizman (Eds.), The structuring of experience. New
    York: Plenum, 1977.

Uzgiris, I.C., & Hunt, J. McV. Assessment in infancy:
    Ordinal scales of psychological development. Urbana,
    IL: University of Illinois Press, 1975.

Wachs, T.D., & Hubert, N.C. Changes in the structure of
    cognitive-intellectual performance during the second
    year of life. Manuscript submitted for publication,
    Purdue University, 1980.

Zachry, W. Ordinality and interdependence of representation
    and language development. Child Development, 1978, 49,
    681-687.

4

PLAY AS PRELINGUISTIC BEHAVIOR: THEORY, EVIDENCE AND APPLICATIONS

Lorraine McCune-Nicolich
Rutgers University

The language specialist has been hampered in recent decades by the lack of a generally accepted and consistent theory of normal language acquisition to guide remediation. Prior to the 1960's an operant learning model of language acquisition prevailed, suggesting operant techniques, emphasizing reinforcement of correct responses, as the treatment of choice in remediating language problems. With the publication of Chomsky's nativist theory, and its extension to language acquisition (McNeill, 1970), the language specialist was faced with the task of teaching behaviors which theory suggested developed on the basis of immutable biological principles. Thus emphasis shifted to teaching the child the specific syntactic structures which were observed in the development of language in normal children.

By the 1970's (e.g., Bloom, 1970, 1973; Braine, 1976; Brown, 1976) emphasis in linguistic theory had shifted to consideration of the cognitive and conceptual bases of language development. Meaning was considered critical in analyzing children's early utterances and in helping language delayed children communicate adequately. In particular, concepts borrowed from Piagetian theory such as attainment of object permanence and the development of means-ends relationships were discussed as cognitive prerequisites to language acquisition. As research evaluating claims that language was correlated with particular sensorimotor tasks was completed (e.g., Bates & Synder, in press; Corrigan, 1978, 1979), it became clear that a simple model specifying the cognitive milestones required for language development was inadequate to account for either the sequence of developments in language acquisition or the individual differences observed.

Language theorists subsequently shifted emphasis from the meanings embodied in language to the functions it served, suggesting that the major prerequisites for language were social rather than cognitive in nature (e.g. Bates, 1976; Halliday, 1975). Aspects of early mother-child interaction, such as turn-taking, were emphasized as precursors

to the communicative aspects of language, and analysis and
intervention began to focus on the child's pragmatic functions rather than on the range of meanings he or she expressed. The role of the language clinician was defined as
enhancing communicative competence rather than developing
either syntactic structures or meanings as had been suggested by earlier models. In practice, however, successful
therapists have continued to emphasize an eclectic model,
attempting to draw on the best that theory has to offer in
developing effective assessment and intervention techniques.

The early 1980's seem to indicate a decade ready for a
rapprochement of the various theories previously developed
to explain language development, possibly resulting in a
multi-dimensional model of acquisition which considers the
cognitive, social and biological aspects of acquisition as a
set of interacting principles, some, but not all of which
are responsive to intervention by the language specialist.
In this chapter, I will (1) describe such a multidimensional model, (2) present preliminary evidence for its
validity, and (3) suggest implications for assessment and
intervention which should be useful to the language clinician working with young language delayed children. In
particular, the relationship of language to symbolization
will be stressed and a method for assessing symbolic development through play observation will be presented.

A Multidimensional Model for Language Acquisition

Language appears to be the most complex behavior of a
two-year old. Its effective use implies (1) biological
principles which allow appropriate maturation of both the
brain and the vocal-articulatory structures, (2) cognitive
principles which allow the construction of meanings, and
(3) social principles which allow the expression of such
meanings in appropriate social contexts. Limitations in any
of these spheres could lead to language delay or disorder.
The model for acquisition to be described here takes as its
basis the hypothesis that cognitive development (conceived
of as a set of internal changes) influences both language
and nonlanguage capabilities. All other things being equal,
corresponding language and nonlanguage skills based on the
same cognitive developments should appear in the child's
behavioral repertoire at approximately the same time.

Thus, if the beginning of mental representation is a cognitive development that allows both the beginnings of pretend play and the establishment word meanings, both of these behaviors should be observed in a child's repertoire at the same time. There is a significant body of literature (e.g., Bates, Camaioni, & Volterra, 1975; Piaget, 1962; Werner & Kaplan, 1963) suggesting that this is the case. However, not every child who exhibits one of these behaviors necessarily exhibits the other. Piaget terms such a lack of correspondence between theoretically corresponding behaviors as decalage. A multidimensional model for language acquisition would attempt to explain decalage in development by appealing to other variables, such as the biological or social bases of language.

For example, in the biological sphere the existence of language abilities in the absence of play abilities would be expected in children with gross motor defects which hampered the child's ability to play freely. Play ability in the absence of corresponding language ability would be expected in children whose vocal-articulatory structures were either deficient or not under appropriate neurological control. In this regard, Ramsay (1980) has shown that the development of a hand preference for bimanual manipulation of objects is accompanied by changes in vocal behavior, such that the child who shows such a preference is also capable of babbling or producing words with differential rather than reduplicated syllables. Both of these changes are used to infer biological reorganization, that is a new level of hemispheric specialization. Lack of such specialization might lead to poor control of the vocal apparatus, and hence a delay in speech as opposed to play.

In the social area, failure to develop appropriate relationships with the mother or primary caregiver might limit the child's motivation to communicate, his or her opportunities for such communication, or for the exercise of a full range of communicative intentions. It is also possible that disturbed mother-child interaction might limit a child's ability or willingness to use the mother as a model for language acquisition.

Nelson (1981) summarized a number of cases of children who apparently used a holistic approach focussing on the

phrase or sentence rather than an analytic approach, focussing on the word in their attempts to learn language. These
children showed poor articulation and a high frequency of
unintelligible speech, suggesting a source of biological
variation. In addition, they showed certain patterns of
mother-child interaction, not characteristic of the majority
of children, suggesting a possible source of social variation. Nelson further reported that some such children
showed a more limited range of pragmatic skills than other
children of comparable developmental levels. Such observed
individual differences may result from a complex interaction
of cognitive, biological and social factors. A multidimensional model of language acquisition should account for such
variation in the normal pattern of development.

The basis for evaluating a multidimensional model of
language acquisition is to specify correspondences between
language and nonlanguage cognitive behaviors, conduct both
longitudinal and cross-sectional investigations to evaluate
the existence of such correspondences, and examine cases of
non-correspondence (or decalage) for the existence of such
external variation (biological or social) as noted above.
McCune-Nicolich (1981b) described the development of symbolization in pretend play and proposed correspondences
between levels of play and language which are summarized in
the following section.

Structure of Early Symbolization

Several lines of research suggest that symbolic play
may be a good predictor of language skill. The sequence of
developments in play is ordinal following the course origi-
nally described by Piaget (1962) and later operationalized
by Nicolich (1977) to include the following five levels:
(1) presymbolic gestures showing understanding of the use of
common objects (e.g., comb, cup, spoon), (2) onset of intentional pretending related to the self, (3) extension of
pretending to include behaviors observed in others and the
use of dolls as participants in play, (4) onset of combinatorial abilities in pretend such that several participants
(e.g., self, doll) are involved with a single action scheme
or several actions are played in sequence, and (5) hierarchically organized play involving evidence that the behavior

was either planned in advance or that a substitute or absent object was used.

Correspondences of language proposed by McCune-Nicolich (1981b) are described as follows. At Level 1 play, both communication and play are pre-symbolic, hence language should exhibit idiosyncratic form and no consistent reference to objects. Thus the child would respond to suggestions such as "wave bye-bye" and use what Dore (1975) has termed phonetically consistent forms (PCF's) to direct adult attention and make requests, but would not use consistent words to refer to specific classes of objects. At Level 2, first referential words, in limited number, variety and frequency of use are expected. The reference of such words would be undifferentiated, appearing to exhibit both over-extension and under-extension in relation to adult language. At Level 3, play exhibits a differentiation of actions from actors and a similar differentiation is proposed for single word vocabularies (Lenneberg, 1975). In particular, relational words, such as "more", "allgone" and "up" (McCune-Nicolich, 1981a) which refer to dynamic relations of entities should occur here.

Two correspondences between play and multi-word language were proposed. At Level 4, when sequences are evident in play, the child should be capable of two simple forms of language combination, routine two-word units that always go together, and pairs of words juxtaposed in relation to the context which give no evidence of organization based on linguistic principles (Lenneberg, 1975; Werner & Kaplan, 1963). At Level 5, when play becomes hierarchically organized, language combinations should increase in frequency and variety as the child develops the capacity for forming linguistic organizational principles as a basis for speech. (Braine, 1976; Maratsos & Chalkley, 1980).

Partial evidence for these correspondences has been provided. A number of studies have reported the co-occurrence of first words with early forms of symbolic play (Bates, Camaioni, & Volterra, 1975; Piaget, 1962; Werner & Kaplan, 1963). Changes in the composition of vocabularies have been observed as stages in language acquisition in many studies but they have not been related to concurrent stages in play (Bates, Benigni, Bretherton, Camaioni, & Volterra, 1979; Nelson, 1973; Werner & Kaplan, 1963). Several studies have reported the predicted correspondences between combinations in language and play milestones (Folger & Leonard, 1978, Hill and McCune-Nicolich, 1981; McCune-Nicolich & Bruskin, in press). In addition, children have been found to rely less on imitation in producing both single words (Nicolich & Raph, 1978) and combinations (Nicolich & Dihoff, 1979) after attaining hierarchically organized symbolic play.

Additional studies have demonstrated correlations between symbolic play and language in both normal and impaired populations (Bates et al., 1975; Bates et al., 1979; Fein, 1978, Fenson & Ramsay, 1980; Inhelder, Lezine, Sinclair & Stambak, 1972, Kahn, 1975; Largo & Howard, 1979; Lowe & Costello, 1976, Sigman & Ungerer, 1980). One study reported improved verbal communication as a result of a symbolic play training (Steckol & Leonard, 1981).

Evaluation of the Multidimensional Model: A Pilot Study

As part of a larger investigation being conducted by the author, 24 subjects between 19 and 24 months of age were evaluated using symbolic play and language measures, as well as measures of hemispheric specialization as indexed by bimanual hand preference (Ramsay, 1980). Qualities of mother-child interaction were also assessed. This study allowed comparison of the development of combinations in play and language and evaluation of the effects of external biological and social variables.

Of the 24 subjects, one exhibited only single symbolic acts (Level 3), 18 exhibited symbolic play combinations (Level 4), and five exhibited both combinations (Level 4) and planning (Level 5) in their play. The subject who showed no combinations in play also failed to combine words. Of 18 subjects showing Level 4 play combinations, 12 produced combinations in language, while six did not. All Level 5 subjects exhibited combinations in both play and language. In addition, four of these five subjects showed a greater proportion of multiword utterances than single word utterances in their language as shown in Table 1. These results provided evidence for two of the original hypotheses. First, the result that all subjects who produced combinations in language also produced play combinations while the subject who produced no play combinations also failed to combine words, supported the prediction that combinations in play would appear in time to combinations in language. Second, since all subjects who exhibited a greater proportion of multiword combinations than single words also showed Level 5 play, the hypothesized relationship between these variables was supported.

Table 1

Subjects Showing Play and Language Combinations

	Child Play Level		
	3	4	5
No Language Combinations	1	6	
Single Words Combinations		12	1
Combinations Single Words			4

The six cases of children who showed combinations in play, but not in language, were relevant to the multi-dimensional model which suggests that cases of noncorrespondence in onset time for language and nonlanguage symbolic behaviors should be interpretable with respect to other variables influencing language. Inspection of the data suggested that these six discrepant cases could be accounted for by measures of mother-child interaction, hemispheric specialization as indexed by bimanual hand preference, and unintelligibility of speech.

Mother-child interaction was assessed in two ways. For 14 subjects, (10 of 12 in the correspondence group and four of six in the decalage group) data from a comprehensive assessment performed by Adler (Note 1), who was unaware of their play level when she performed her coding, were available. For all 24 subjects in the study frequency with which children shared objects with their mothers in a play session (giving and showing) was scored. Adler's results indicated that a certain constellation of negative behaviors characterized discordant mother-child interactions. Subjects in the decalage and correspondence groups were identified who showed one or more of these negative behaviors or who were in the lowest quartile for frequency of sharing with their mothers.

Intelligibility of language was assessed by a measure of the frequency of intelligible and unintelligible utterances produced by the subject. Subjects who exhibited a greater proportion of intelligible than unintelligible utterances were characterized as intelligible, while those who produced a number of unintelligible utterances equal to or greater than their intelligible utterances were characterized as unintelligible.

Separate Fisher exact tests revealed that the decalage group was characterized by a significantly greater number of children exhibiting unintelligibility of speech ($p < .004$) and more negative characteristics of mother-child interaction ($p < .004$) than the correspondence group (Tables 2 and 3). There was no significant difference between the groups in presence or absence of a hand preference.

Table 2

Number of Subjects Showing Unintelligible Language
in Correspondence and Decalage Groups

	Intelligible	Unintelligible
Correspondence	10	2
Decalage	0	6

Table 3

Number of Subjects Showing Negative Mother-Child Interaction
for Correspondence and Decalage Groups

	Mother-Child Interaction	
	No Negative Characteristics	Negative Characteristics
Correspondence	9	3
Decalage	0	6

Comparison of Language at Level 4 and Level 5

Comparisons were made between Level 4 and Level 5 subjects on several language variables using t tests. As hypothesized, the proportion of multiword types to total intelligible utterances was greater for the Level 5 group (.64), than for the Level 4 group who exhibited combinations in their language (.45) (p < .005). The Level 5 subjects also exhibited greater mean MLU (1.6 vs. 1.3, p < .05) which replicates the findings of a previous longitudinal study (McCune-Nicholich & Bruskin, in press).

Influence of Handedness

Inspection of the results for hand preference revealed that subjects failing to exhibit a hand preference fell into two distinct groups such that the effect of this variable on the other analyses was obscured. Of nine children failing to show a hand preference, four were characterized by Level 5 play and the advanced performance in language associated with that level, one exhibited both language and play combinations in her repertoire. The remaining four subjects were characterized by a lack of combinations in both play and language or a lack of combinations only in language. In addition, these four subjects exhibited a preponderance of

unintelligible speech, and the lowest performance in language observed in this sample. These anomalous results were
not helpful in clarifying the relationship between hemispheric specialization and language maturity.

Intelligibility

     In addition to analysis of differences in intelligi-
bility between correspondence and decalage groups described
above, two additional analyses were performed. Separate
Fisher exact tests revealed that intelligibility and poor
mother-child interaction were closely associated (p < .0001)
as were intelligibility and characterization of the child as
high or low on language maturity according to weighted ranks
of MLU, vocabulary size and frequency of speech (p < .0001).
These findings are seen in Tables 4 and 5, respectively.
These results are in accord with predictions by Nelson
(1981) suggesting that poor intelligibility, disturbed
mother-child interaction and slow language development,
along with additional variables characterize a style of
language acquisition exhibited by a minority of children
described in the language literature.

Table 4

Number of Subjects Showing Unintelligible Language
and Problems in Mother-Child Interaction

	Intelligible	Unintelligible
M-C Interaction		
No Problems	14	0
Problems	1	8

Table 5

Subjects Showing Unintelligible Language and Low
Language Maturity

		Intelligible	Unintelligible
	High	15	0
Language Maturity			
	Low	0	8

While it may be tempting to assume that poor mother-child interaction functions as a cause of language deviation, this inference is not justified by these data. It is equally possible that interaction with a child who is slow in developing language leads mothers to develop unusual approaches to interaction with their children. Such underlying variables as delay in hemispheric specialization for language or delay in symbolic development may underlie a variety of language problems, as may inappropriate mother-child interaction patterns.

On the basis of preliminary data available, it seems that use of a symbolic play assessment as part of the evaluation of a language delayed preschooler is warranted. The pretend play context also provides valuable opportunties for enhancing symbolization and language which can be exercised by the language specialist. In the following sections, an approach to symbolic play assessment and suggestions for using play to improve language will be discussed.

Symbolic Play Assessment

The desirable context for assessing play is a secure, comfortable setting, which puts as few constraints as pos-

sible on the child's behavior. Consequently, play at home
with the mother is recommended. In a laboratory setting the
room should be as comfortable and homelike as possible. The
session should be videotaped if possible. Adequate famil-
iarization with the examiner and video equipment is essential. The mother should behave as naturally as possible in
responding to the child, but avoid making specific suggestions about what to do with the toys. The examiner should
not interact with mother or child during the session.

Mother and child are seated on the floor and a bucket
of toys (Table 6) is placed near them. After twenty minutes
of taping, the session is interrupted. The bucket is over-
turned and a subset of toys which has been shown to elicit
symbolic play is arranged. The wrapped baby doll, cup,
plate, spoon, teapot and cover, brush and comb, mirror,
purse, doll bottle and cloth are placed on top of the pile.
The monkey doll, girl doll, dump truck and telephone are
placed in front of the bucket. Taping proceeds without
further interruption.

If possible a written transcript of the session should
be prepared. The transcript is then divided into units
termed "episodes". Each episode is then assigned the appropriate play levels listed in Appendix A. Finally a summary
assessment of the child's symbolic play performance can be
prepared.

Establishing play episodes

Many coding systems rely on time sampling or time devi-
sions to break the stream of behavior into codeable units.
Such divison is unlikely to follow the naturally occurring
behavioral transitions exhibited by the participants. The
present system attempts to divide the stream of behavior in
a way that preserves the participant generated organization
of activities.

An episode can be generally defined as: 1) a single
object contact or 2) continuous involvement with a group of
objects, which together form a "theme" for the child. An
episode begins when the child has nothing in hand, continues
as he or she contacts an object and ends when the child is
again empty-handed. The child may pick up and play with

Table 6

Toy List[1]

11	Blanket - doll is wrapped in	32	Jeep - toy
12	Blocks	33	Mailtruck - Fisher-Price
13	Book - Baby's Things	34	Match-box - sliding
14	Book - Pat the Bunny	35	Mirror - Small
15	Brush - Small	36	Mop - toy
16	Comb - Large	37	Monkey - 7" Stuffed
17	Comb - Small	38	Napkin - cloth
18	Cup - toy	39	Nipple Cover
19	Saucer - toy	40	Necklace - white plastic
*20	Doll - Baby	*41	Nesting cups - round
*22	Doll baby's clothes: diaper, jacket & bonnet and wrapped in blanket.	42	Ping Pong Ball
		*43	Popbeads - snapped in necklace
*21	Doll - Ginny Doll	44	Purse - toy
*22	Ginny doll's clothes: blue pants, red jacket with hood, red shoes	*45	Puzzle with five pieces: chicken, pig, mule, cow, duck
		46	Scrubbrush
23	Doll Bottle with soft nipple	47	Slippers - pair of women's
24	Dog - Dakin Brown Stuffed	48	Sponge

Table 6 (cont.)

25	Drum with bell inside	49	Sunglasses - Child's - lenses removed
25	Drum with bell inside	*50	Teapot - toy
26	Dumbo Jack-in-the-box	*51	Teapot cover - toy
*27	Dumping Bottle - clear plastic milk bottle	52	Teaspoon
		53	Telephone - toy
*28	Dumping bottle pieces: apple, grapes, banana, lemon, doll bottle, two fish, butter, milk, orange juice, red bottle, corn	*54	Toolbox - toy
		*55	Tools - Toy: hammer, screwdriver, wrench, saw pliers
29	Finger puppet - Grover	56	Truck - 12"
30	Finger puppet - Oscar	57	Man - 2" Fisher-Price
31	Iron - toy		

*Those items which are presented as unit.

[1]A more complete list may be obtained by writing to the author

additional objects without terminating the episode. As long as (a) the original object remains in hand, or (b) a theme of action unifies the child's activities, the episode continues.

Example:

> Child is playing (dialing, talking) with toy phone. With receiver to shoulder, the child puts in a puzzle piece, picks up the pop beads, then talks on the phone again, and finally puts phone down.

Child sits with doll nearby, picks up doll bottle,
feeds doll, puts down bottle. Child picks up
blanket, covers doll, saying "nite-nite". Then
moves to another activity.

Child grooms self with three objects (e.g., two
combs and a brush), setting each aside after it is
used.

Some objects, those presented to the child as a unit,
ordinarily function as a unit in defining episodes. These
items are starred in Table 6. They include coffee pot
w/lid, baby doll w/clothing, pop-beads, building cups,
little girl doll w/clothing, puzzle w/pieces, tool box
w/tools, clear milk bottle w/pretend foods.

Coding Symbolic Play

In categorizing the symbolic play level of an activity,
a number of discrete judgments is made concerning the
child's behavior. A flow chart (Table 7) has been designed
to facilitate these decisions. This flow chart presents a
series of questions, the answers to which determine the
level of the activity observed. In using the chart consider
questions 1-4 in order. If the answer to any of these
questions is "no," make note of the level designated and
stop. If question 4 is answered "yes," consider all of the
following questions (5-7).

Criteria for Level 1. Is there socialized object use?
Certain objects have very definite uses which the child is
likely to observe in his or her daily life. These involve
appropriate use of everyday objects (e.g., a spoon used for
eating or feeding, a comb used for grooming rather than both
used for banging).

Code NO, if such behavior is not observed.

Code YES, if the child demonstrates knowledge of such uses
by appropriate gesture. (Note: These gestures may be
extremely brief. Examples: Put doll bottle, cup or spoon
to mouth, put comb or brush to hair, roll truck or car along
floor, push iron along surface, put mop to floor and
"swish.")

Table 7

Flow Chart for Assigning Symbolic Play Levels
Within an Episode

| | Level | Assigned |
| | Yes | No |

1. Is there a socialized object use?
    If no ------------------------------   0
    If yes: continue

2. Is there evidence of pretending:
    If no ------------------------------   1
    If yes: continue

3. Is the action decentered? i.e.:
    a)   using objects/people as partici-
         pants?
    b)   learned by observation of others?
    If no ------------------------------   2
    If yes: continue

4. If the scheme repeated more than
    once with different participants or
    is more than one scheme involved?
    If no ------------------------------   3
    If yes: continue
    a)   is a single scheme repeated with
         different participants or differ-
         ent objects? ------------------   4.1
    b)   is more than one scheme
         demonstrated? ------------------   4.2

5. Is any scheme planned? -------------   5.1
    Is any definitive object substitution
    observed? ------------------------   5.1

    Is the Level 5.1 behavior part of
    a 4.0, 4.1, or 4.2 episode?
    If so ------------------------------   5.2

Criteria for Level 2.   Is there evidence of pretending?

Code NO, if no such evidence is observed and code play behavior as Level 1.

Code YES, if:

(a) inanimate objects are treated as animate (e.g. care-
     taking of doll)

(b) activities performed in absence of the necessary mate-
     rials (e.g. drink from empty cup).

(c) child performs actions usually done by someone else
     (e.g., cooking, telephoning).

(d) activities are not carried to their usual outcome
     (e.g., purse over arm, wave, but not go out).

(e) one object is substituted for another (e.g., shell =
     cat).

The assumption is made that the child is aware of the dual
quality of this behavior, i.e., the juxtaposition of a real
action and intended fantasy (Dunn & Wooding, 1977; Fein,
1975; Nicolich, 1977).   The child's "playful" attitude may
influence this decision.

Important: Pretend play can occur without the use of
any objects.   If evidence of pretend is observed, continue
through the flow chart until the appropriate level is
reached.

Criteria for Level 3.   Is   the   action   decentered?

Code NO, if: pretending is limited to a single enactment of
a usual "baby activity" applied to the self. Code this play
behavior as Level 2.   Examples: brush own hair, pretend to
sleep, pretend to eat or drink.

Code YES, if:

(a) the child applies an action normally done with respect
     to his or her own body to a toy (often doll or stuffed
     animal) or to the mother (e.g., feeding, grooming,
     sleeping, toileting, etc.).

(b)   The child does an action normally performed by someone
      else (e.g., pretend mop, hammer, read, "dress-up" with
      purse, etc.).

Code this play behavior as Level 3.

    Criteria for Level 4.   Is the scheme (a) repeated more
than once with different participants or (b) is more than
one action scheme involved?

Code NO, if: a single action and actor are involved, even
if the identical behavior is repeated several times.   Code
this play behavior as Level 2 or 3 (see above criteria).

Code YES, if:

(a)   the same scheme is repeated with two or more partici-
      pants (e.g., feed self, feed doll).   Code this play
      behavior as Level 4.

(b)   more than one scheme is played with the same or dif-
      ferent objects.   Code this play behavior as Level 4.

    Criteria for Level 5.   Is any scheme planned or any
substitute object used?   Behavior coded here should be based
more on the child's mental construction of a pretend game
than on the perceptual or functional characteristics of
objects.

Code NO, if: no planned schemes are observed.

Code YES, if:

(a)   there is verbal announcement (even a single word) prior
      to the action (e.g., the child has the doll in hand,
      says "feed" or "bottle" and uses the bottle or some
      other object to feed the doll) or

(b)   there is directed search for the materials needed for
      the game (e.g., the child has the doll in hand,
      searches through the basket, discarding several toys,
      finds the bottle and feeds the doll) or

(c)   a clearly unusual object is used to perform some acti-
      vity.   It is assumed here that the child is aware of

the ordinary object to be used and is making an <u>inten-</u><u>tional</u> substitution. Ideal evidence is of two types: either verbal annoucement of the substitution or use of the object in more than one action (e.g., use toy screwdriver to feed doll <u>and</u> to "fix" tool box or "swim" like a fish.) Sometimes the obvious disparity between the "substitute object" and its usual counter- part can serve as a criterion (e.g., drink from block; feed doll with screwdriver).

Summarizing the Child's Symbolic Play Performance

The child's performance can be categorized using the highest level of play consistently and independently ob- served. Observation of two behaviors involving different objects, neither of which was modeled or suggested by the mother is the minimum criterion for assigning an overall level to the child for that session. It also may be of interest to consider the child's modal level and the dis- tribution of activities across the levels. The content of the child's play should be evaluated also. At a given level the child may perseverate, using only a few activities repeatedly, such as feeding self, doll, examiner; or the child may exhibit rich variation in schemes and combina- tions, perhaps including baby care, housekeeping, telephone and puppet play all within a given session. Both level of play and range of meanings expressed in play can be used in planning play-based interventions.

Play As A Context For Language Therapy

Play-based interventions are necessarily child-centered. Participation must be voluntary, and the child's focus of interest forms the basis for the therapist's subtle guidance in developmentally positive directions. Johnson, Dowling and Wesner (1980) of the Milwaukee Child and Adolescent Treatment Center have developed a technique termed Infant and Toddler Centered Activity which provides a framework both for enhancing the child's ability to initiate communi- cation with others, and an opportunity for the therapist to activate his or her agenda for more specific developmental improvements. McCune-Nicolich and Carroll (1981) summarized suggestions for adapting this technique for work with young language delayed children.

1. Prepare for the play session by "child-proof-
    ing" a room or area so that there should be
    no need to prohibit the child from any acti-
    vity.

2. Assemble a few toys (appropriate types and
    number depend on the child's maturity) which
    will form a focus for the session.

3. Avoid having specific expectations for the
    child's performance. Instead, allow the
    child to take the lead in choice of toys and
    activities.

4. Sit on the floor near the child, watching and
    waiting for an invitation to join in play.
    Try to become aware of what the child is
    trying to do and facilitate these intentions.
    Never "take over" for the child; rather
    remain in the role of supportive partner.

5. Be aware that child centered play sessions
    are a special situation, not typical of
    routine teacher-child interactions. If it is
    necessary to resume a directive role, end the
    session.

At this point, with the child comfortably in control of
him or herself, and the immediate situation, opportunities
for encouraging play and language behaviors at, or slightly
above the child's observed level can begin. However, at
every step of the way it is necessary to monitor the child's
involvement in and reaction to the session. Language acquisition, like toilet-training can become a battleground for
the two or three-year old striving to actualize his or her
own autonomy. By allowing the child freedom to communicate
without pressure, one may avoid such conflicts. This technique is most appropriate for use with young children (below
the age of three years) but can be modified to accommodate
older children. Rather than replacing more traditional
language therapies, Infant/Toddler Centered Activity can be
used to supplement an ongoing program. In addition, following the model provided by Johnson et al., parents can be
trained as therapists to use play sessions as simple opportunities for closeness and communication. Such a home

program benefits the child's more formal language therapy by enhancing symbolic and communicative development in general and by providing greater opportunity for exercise of these developing abilities.

How can the creative clinician bring his or her goals for the child into the type of session described without taking over the session and violating its character? This is no easy task. The clinician is limited here to means of preparing the environment (e.g., certain toys lead to certain forms of conversation and concept development), and learning how to integrate a therapeutic agenda into the child's plan of action. The first step is to observe the child closely enough so that preference for toys and activities can be predicted. The second is to develop a broad range of goals for the child, so that a given objective is likely to come to mind as the child engages in a particular activity. A few simple examples follow.

Suppose you notice that the child enjoys puzzles, blocks, and container play. A broad agenda for language facilitation might include "comprehension and production of prepositions" as well as "development of an action verb vocabulary."

As the child plays, opportunities arise for labelling particular actions: "fit" the piece; "drop" the block; and relationships: the block is "in" the container; the small block is "on" the large block. Similarly, language production can be stimulated by entering into interactive games with the child where the therapist responds to the child's requests such as "Put the block in the box.", or "Put the piece in the space." Similar commands can be encouraged with questions such as "Where shall I put the block?"

Pretend play has been considered a useful vehicle for extending a child's symbolic capacity. The child who shows little inclination to such play can be encouraged by provision of appropriate toys and modeling of such symbolic acts as appropriate use of common objects and pretend play with dolls or miniatures such as the Fisher-Price Adventure People. Children are as fascinated by watching an adult demonstrate pretend play as they are with listening to stories. Modeling play with reluctant children both increases the frequency of such play and allows demonstration of the highest levels of symbolic functioning of which the child is capable (Fenson & Ramsay, 1981). The use of pretend play as a stimulus for language development is only beginning (Steckol & Leonard, 1981); the possibilities remain to be explored and extended.

REFERENCE NOTE

1.   Adler, L. Quality of mother-child interaction in rela-
     tion to play and cognitive. Dissertation, in pre-
     paration, Rutgers University.

REFERENCES

Bates, E. Language and context. New York: Academic Press,
     1976.

Bates, E. & Synder, L. The cognitive hypothesis in language
     development. In I. Uzgiris & J. McV. Hunt (Eds.),
     Research with scales of psychological development in
     infancy. Champaign-Urbana: University of Illinois
     Press, in press.

Bates, E., Camaioni, L., & Volterra, V. The acquisition of
     performatives prior to speech. Merrill Palmer Quarter-
     ly, 1975, 21(3), 205-225.

Bloom, L. One word at a time: The use of single word utter-
     ances before syntax. The Hague: Mouton, 1973, P. 261.

Bloom, L. Language develoment: Form and function in emerg-
     ing grammars. Cambridge, Mass.: M.I.T. Press, 1970.

Braine, M. Children's first word combinations. Monographs
     of the Society for Research in Child Development, 1976,
     41 (1, Serial No. 164).

Brown, R. A first language: The early stages. Cambridge,
     Mass: Harvard University Press, 1973.

Corrigan, R. Cognitive correlates of language: Differen-
     tial criteria yield differential results. Child Devel-
     opment, 1979, 50, 617-631.

Corrigan, R. Language development as related to stage 6 object permanence development. Journal of Child Language, 1978, 5(2).

Dore, J. Holophrases, speech acts and language universals. Journal of Child Language, 1975, 2, 21-39.

Dunn, J. & Wooding, C. Play in the home and its implications for learning. In B. Tizard & D. Harvey (Eds.), Biology of Play. Philadelphia: Pa.: J.B. Lippincott, 1977.

Fein, G. Play revisited. In M. Lamb (Ed.), Social and Personality Development. New York: Holt, Rinehart & Winston, 1978.

Fein, G. A transformational analysis of pretending. Developmental Psychology, 1975, 11(3), 291-296.

Fenson, L. and Ramsay, D. Decentration and integration of play in the second year of life. Child Development, 1980, 51, 171-178.

Fenson, L. & Ramsay, D. Effects of modeling action sequences on the play of twelve-, fifteen-, and nineteen-month-old children. Child Development, 1981, 52(3), 1028-1036.

Folger, K.M. & Leonard, L.B. Language and sensorimotor behavior during the early period of referential speech. Journal of Speech and Hearing Research, 1978, 21, 519-527.

Halliday, M.A.K. Learning how to mean. In E.H. Lenneberg & E. Lenneberg (Eds.), Foundations of language development: A multidisciplinary approach, Vol. 1. New York: Academic Press, 1975.

Hill, P.M. & McCune-Nicolich, L. Pretend play and patterns of cognition in Down's syndrome children. Child Development, 1981, 52(2), 611-617.

Inhelder, B., Lezine, I., Stambak, M., & Sinclair-de Zwart. Les debuts de la function semiotique. Archives de Psychologie, 1972, 163 (XLI), 187-243.

Johnson, F.K., Dowling, J., & Wesner, D. Notes on infant psychotherapy. Infant Mental Health Journal, 1980, 1(1), 19-33.

Kahn, J.V. Relationship of Piaget's sensorimotor period to language acquisition of profoundly retarded children. American Journal of Mental Deficiency, 1975, 6, 640-643.

Largo, R.M. & Howard, J.A. Developmental progression in play behavior of children between nine and thirty months: II: Spontaneous play in language development. Develop. Med. Child Neurol., 1979, 21, 492-503.

Lenneberg, E. The concept of language differentiation. In E.H. Lenneberg & E. Lenneberg, E. (Eds.), Foundations of language development: A multi-disciplinary approach. New York: Academic Press, 1975.

Lowe, M. & Costello, A. Manual for the symbolic play test (experimental edition). London: NFER Publishing Co., Ltd., 1976.

Maratos, M.P. & Chalkley, M.A. The internal language of children's syntax: The ontogenisis and representation of syntactic categories. In K. Nelson (Ed.), Children's Language, Vol. 2. New York: Gardner Press, 1980.

McCune-Nicolich, L. The cognitive bases of relational words in the single word period. Journal of Child Language, 1981a, 8, 15-34.

McCune-Nicholich, L. Toward symbolic functioning: Structure of early pretend games and potential parallels with language. Child Development, 1981b, 52, 785-797.

McCune-Nicholich, L. & Bruskin, C. Combinatorial competency in play and language. In K. Rubin & D. Pepler (Eds.), The Play of Children: Current Theory and Research. Basel, Switzerland: S. Karger, in press.

McCune-Nicholich, L. & Carrol, S. Development of Symbolic Play: Implications for the language specialist. Topics in Language Disorders, 1981, 1-15.

McNeill, D. The acquisition of language. New York: Harper & Rowe, 1970.

Nelson, K. Individual differences in language development: Implications for development and language. Developmental Psychology, 1981, 17, 170-187.

Nelson, K. Structure and strategy in learning to talk. Monographs of the Society for Research in Child Development, 1973, 38 (1-2, Serial No. 149).

Nicolich, L. McCune. Beyond sensorimoter intelligence: Assessment of symbolic maturity through analysis of pretend play. Merrill-Palmer Quarterly, 1977, 23(2), 89-101.

Nicolich, L. & Dihoff, R. Early word combinations: Syntax, semantics or something simpler. Paper presented at the Boston Language Conference, 1979.

Nicolich, L. McCune & Raph, J. Imitative language and symbolic maturity in the single word period. Journal of Psycholinguistic Research, 1978, 7, 401-417.

Piaget, J. Play, dreams and imitation. New York: Norton, 1962.

Ramsay, D.S. Beginnings of bimanual handedness and speech in infants. Infant Behavior and Development, 1980, 3, 67-77.

Sigman, M. & Ungerer, J. Sensorimotor skills and language comprehension in autistic children. Unpublished Manuscript, UCLA, 1980.

Steckol, K. & Leonard, L. Sensorimotor development and the use of prelinguistic performatives. Journal of Speech and Hearing Research, 1981, 24, 262-268.

Werner, H., & Kaplan, B. Symbol formation. New York: Wiley, 1963.

Appendix A

Sequence of Symbolic Levels According to Piaget and as Applied in this Research

Piaget (1962)	Nicolich Levels and Criteria	Examples
Sensorimoter Period		
Prior to Stage VI	(1) Presymbolic Scheme: The child shows understanding of object use of meaning by brief recognitory gestures. No pretending. Properties of present object are the stimulus Child appears serious rather than playful.	The child picks up a comb, touches it to his hair, drops it. The child picks up the telephone receiver, puts it into ritual conversation position, sets it aside. The child gives the mop a swish on the floor.
Stage VI	(2) Auto-symbolic Scheme: The child pretends at self-related activities. Pretending Symbolism is directly involved with the child's body. Child appears playful, seems aware of pretending.	The child simulates drinking from a toy baby bottle. The child eats from an empty spoon. The child closes his eyes, pretending to sleep.
Symbolic Stage I	(3) Single Scheme Symbolic Games (Child extends symbolism beyond his own actions by:	
Type I A Assimilative	A. Including other actors or receivers of action, such as doll or mother.	Child feeds mother or doll (A). Child grooms mother or doll (A).
Type I B Imitative	B. Pretending at activities of other people or objects such as dogs, trucks, trains, etc.	Child pretends to read a book (B). Child pretends to mop floor (B). Child moves a block or toy car with appropriate sounds of vehicle (B).

Appendix A (Cont.)

Piaget (1962)	Nicolich Levels and Criteria	Examples
	Symbolic Stage I (Cont.)	
These distinctions are not made by Piaget	(4) Combinatorial Symbolic Games	Child combs own, then mothers's hair.
	4.1 Single Scheme Combinations: one pretend scheme is related to several actors or receivers of action.	Child drinks from the bottle, feeds doll from bottle. (4.1)
		Child puts an empty cup to mother's mouth, then experimenter, and self. (4.1)
	4.2 Multi-scheme combinations: Several schemes are related to one another in sequence.	Child holds phone to ear, dials.
		Child kisses doll, puts it to bed, puts spoon to its mouth. (4.2)
		Child stirs in the pot, feeds doll, pours food into dish. (4.2)
	(5) Planned Symbolic Games: Child indicates verbally or non-verbally that pretend acts are planned before being executed.	Child finds the iron, sets it down, searches for the cloth, tossing aside several objects. When cloth is found, she irons it. (5.1)
	5.1 Planned Single Scheme Symbolic Acts Transitional Type: Activities from levels 2-3 that are planned.	Child picks up play screw-driver, says "tooth-brush" and makes the motions of tooth-brushing. (5.1)
Type II A	Type A Symbolic identification of one object with another.	
Type II B	Type B Symbolic identification of the child's body with some other person or object.	Child picks up the bottle, says "baby," then feeds the doll and covers it with a cloth. (5.2)
Type III A	5.2 Combinations with Planned Elements These are constructed of activities from Levels 2-5.1, but always include some planned element. They tend toward realistic scenes.	Child puts play foods in a pot, stirs them. Then says "soup" or "Mommy" before feeding the mother. She waits, then says "more?" offering the spoon to the mother. (5.2)

81

5

COMMUNICATION STRATEGIES
FOR LANGUAGE INTERVENTION

James D. MacDonald
Nisonger Center
The Ohio State University

Introduction and Background

For ten years, students and I have struggled with the task of bridging a striking gap between ourselves and hundreds of handicapped children.1 That gap was communication. Many of these children who had some expressive language acted as though they did not know what to do with their language. As we came to know them, we found that these children nearly always knew much more than they communicated; thus to have relied on traditional structural approaches to language would have led to severe underestimation of their cognitive and social competencies. Thus, until these children communicated more and until we learned to assess their communication as well as language, we would continue to underestimate their knowledge and ignore the essential communicative bases of language (Bates, 1976; Bruner, 1978b; Lewis and Lee-Painter, 1972; Moerk, 1977; and Snow, 1972).

Our own clinical experiences, literature searches, and research programs (Almerico & MacDonald, 1978; Lombardino, 1978; Lombardino, Willems and MacDonald, 1980; MacDonald and Blott, 1974; MacDonald, Blott, Gordon & Spiegel, 1974; MacDonald and Horstmeier, 1978; Nichols, 1975; and Owens, 1978) have led us to the overwhelming conclusion that if we are to understand and alter the children's primary social, cognitive, and linguistic competencies we must find ways to help the children establish conversational systems within which these competencies can be both revealed and developed.

The intervention model to be reported in this paper is being developed at the Ohio State University in the clinical, training and research context of the Nisonger Center2 which is a graduate training center where students of several disciplines learn to become specialists in educating developmentally delayed individuals. Specifically, these language programs have developed out of three contexts:

weekly evaluations with the families of developmentally delayed children of all diagnoses; two preschool and two infant education classes each integrated with children ranging from normally developing to severely and multiply handicapped; and parent-based language training programs.

In 1971, the language program at the Center began to develop assessment and training approaches in response to two basic questions: What kinds of expressive language should first be taught? And, how should that teaching take place? In response to these problems, we developed an intervention approach that used the well established semantic approach to grammar (Brown, 1973; MacDonald, 1978; and Schlesinger, 1971) as the content bases for first sentences rather than the traditional structural (syntax) and conceptual (e.g. color, shape, and size) approaches. The semantic approach offered targets that occurred naturally in the child's sensorimotor and social world. The Environmental Language Intervention (ELI) Program (Horstmeier and MacDonald, 1978a). developed from this semantic base and extended to prelinguistic skills needed for development of the child's early meanings.

The problem of "how to teach" language was approached by exploring ways for generalization to natural use. The problem of generalizing language gains has received widespread attention, particularly from systematic, criterion based behaviorial approaches. Harris (1974), in her extensive review of over 200 studies on language generalization, concluded that much work remained to solve the problem of efficient natural generalization.

Our early clinical experiences revealed that when we taught parents specific strategies for facilitating language, their children showed more generalized gains than did similar children who received therapy in the classroom (MacDonald, 1978; MacDonald et. al., 1974; Mechlenberg, 1976; Nichols, 1975). Consequently, Deanna Horstmeier and I began a series of parent-assisted programs directed to training initial sentences and prelinguistic skills (Horstmeier and MacDonald, 1978b).

During the years that we field-tested the language model (ELI) in evaluations as well as classroom and parent programs, we became aware of new directions needed for spontaneous generalization of language learning. A series of clinical findings from the parent and classroom programs resonated well current research and theory from several professional fields. The following clinical - theoretical - research problems formed the impetus for a new model for language intervention.

A major finding of our work was that language training effects appeared to generalize in some children but not in others. The discrepancy appeared to be related to several factors, all of which influenced our direction in developing the current model.

First, those children who showed most language gains were those who had a primary conversational system with their significant others (SOs). We came to see that those having no reciprocal turntaking relationships (i.e. conversational) had no generalization mechanism through which they could naturally practice their new skills. These clinical findings were supported strongly in the theoretical and research literature in parent-child interactions (Bruner, note 2; Lewis and Rosenblum, 1974; Moerk, 1976; Snow, 1972) and pragmatics (Bates, 1976; Dore, 1975) which have concluded that language develops from early nonlinguistic conversations and joint activities between the child and his significant others.

We continued to see in our families of handicapped children that didactic, caretaking and noncontingent parallel patterns appeared to characterize the relationships between the child and his parent or teacher. We came to see a strikingly consistent behavioral profile in the parents and teachers for whom the model is intended:

1) They often talk in long sentences, thus mismatching the child's communicative competence.

2) They communicate frequently without the child's attention to topic.

3) They communicate "rhetorically," that is, with little waiting or cueing for a response.

4) They act as though they do not expect the child to communicate.

5) They accomodate to the child's idiosyncratic communica-
    tion instead of shaping his behavior to more conven-
    tional performance.

6) They assume that the professionals in language training
    are in a better position than they to improve their
    child's communication.

These behavioral profiles of parents and teachers placed the
child in a noncontingent receiving role, rather than in the
active participant role needed for language learning
(Bruner, note 1; Hunt, 1961). Or, they may place the child
in a lead role and not shape toward a conventional system.
Consequently we decided that the cornerstone to a new approach would have to be conversation, that is, the reciprocal and differentially contingent turntaking relationship
that nearly all mothers have with their infants (Lewis and
Rosenblum, 1974). As we consistently observed minimal
feedback that adults appear to get from a handicapped child,
we suspected that the child had, in effect, naturally
trained those adults to interact in didactic and caretaking
ways. The model proposed here is an attempt to reestablish
the natural and reciprocal teaching relationship that is
assumed to have existed in infancy. To do this, the child's
parents and teachers must take the dual role of client and
teacher. They must learn to behave in ways that contingently match the child's current communication system. They
must be communicators.

A second major issue in the model's development came in
part from our finding that most handicapped children have an
idiosyncratic communication system with their significant
others that is neither understood nor accepted by strangers.
While teaching expressive language in the earlier programs,
we found that we were competing with a nonlinguistic idiosyncratic vocal or nonvocal system which worked well for the
child. His family and peers had learned to reinforce his
special ways of sending messages, failing to reinforce more
conventional communication attempts. Concurrent with this
awareness, we studied communication theory (Bateson &
Jackson, 1964; Haley, 1964; Jackson, 1968; Watzlawick,
Beavin & Jackson, 1967) and came to realize that all behaviors can communicate and that we had previously been attending only to communications that were conventional
(understood and accepted by strangers within a culture).

Thus, here we were teaching words a few times a week, while often the child's body language and other idiosyncratic behaviors were being maintained by strong natural reinforcers. Consequently, we began to develop an approach that recognized all behaviors as potentially communicative and that placed the SOs in a state of contingent responsiveness given that the child learns to communicate in terms of the effects his behavior has on the environment (Skinner, 1953).

Consistent with these two issues, we found that it was relatively easy to train parents and teachers to carry out didactic lessons, but much more difficult to extend the principles to spontaneous training necessary for generalization. Our new awareness of pragmatics and parent-child interaction principles hit head-on with our discomfort with the didactic teaching we saw pervading the child's relationships with family and classroom. Emerging research and theory argued that functional language use could develop only in spontaneous, child-oriented joint activities (Bruner, note 2; Snow, 1972). Thus we had to reassess the basic therapy model that had been used. Note that the profession of speech pathology had developed a model of therapy that was a one-to-one brief encounter with one client isolated from his natural environment. Such a model was developed with individuals who already had the conversation skills which they could use in generalizing what they learned in therapy. However, most handicapped children I have known do not have a well-habituated conversational system; in other words, when we teach these children language skills they have no natural place to go to generalize.

Many other clinical, theoretical and research issues will be discussed throughout the paper. What I intend to do in this paper is to introduce three aspects of an emerging model. First, I discuss the background of the model in terms of five theoretical perspectives; ecological theory of child development, communication theory, pragmatics (interactive psycholinguistics), operant theory, and systems theory. These theories have been very helpful in organizing years of clinical observations and research findings. Second, I present the three classifications of behavioral targets for intervention: conversation, child and significant other person. I have attempted to present the emerging taxonomy in terms of clinical strategies as we apply them. And third, I discuss in detail the design of a curriculum that is used within homes and classrooms.

Theoretical, Research and Clinical Background of the Model

The model has evolved through a continuous integration of clinical events with research and theoretical findings from several disciplines. As we were developing a system for building language-facilitating conversations, several disciplines were concurrently providing a support structure that has helped to anchor the model solidly in independently developed findings. Although no one theoretical approach to language development has yet to integrate the necessary content and process concerns into a single design for clinical implementation, certain research bases did resonate well with our findings of ten years in home and classroom based programs. Our overriding goal came to be language through conversation, and we searched for theoretical concepts and research findings that might provide a bridge from a child's knowledge of language to his use of it in conversation. Five theoretical approaches will be presented primarily in terms of their primary implications for the content and design of the current model.

Communication Theory

A group of scholars and clinicians (Bateson and Jackson, 1964; Bateson, Jackson, Haley, and Weakland, 1966; Haley, 1962, 1964; Jackson, 1962; Jackson and Weakland, 1961; Watzlawick, Beavin and Jackson, 1967;) have studied communication disorders in adults for over 30 years. Their resultant pragmatic theory of communication and their research findings offer valuable directions to our work with children. Three of the primary principles of this theory are 1) every behavior, regardless of form or intention, can communicate, i.e. send a message; 2) communication is a cybernetic phenomenon, i.e. one that functions as a feedback loop between members of a dyad who reciprocally affect each other; and 3) expectancy in the form of a self-fulfilling prophecy plays a vital role in determining the ways others communicate.

Briefly now, how do these principles influence the design of language intervention? The first principle, that every behavior can communicate, addresses the problem of the basic units to be assessed and trained. Most traditional and even recent pragmatic, approaches to language training limit themselves to verbal linguistic units and to other

behaviors judged as intending to communicate. In our clinical work, we have become aware that handicapped children
frequently send effective messages with primitive signals
and behaviors that are idiosyncratic to the particular child
and significant other (SO). Thus, we decided to select as
the basic units for training any behaviors that effectively
send messages to others. Thus, communication is defined in
terms of its effects on others, not in terms of any predetermined units such as phoneme, word, syntactic unit or
other units representing "linguistic" approaches to the
training task. Related to the issue of basic units is the
frequent observation that many of the behaviors that effectively communicate a message to a child's significant others
(persons familiar to him) do not do so with strangers.
Through familiarity with the form and context, parents and
teachers learn to decode the child's idiosyncratic communications. Strangers, such as clinicians and psychological
evaluators thus, see much less of the child's behavior as
communicative. This principle, then, urges us to consider
all behaviors as potential steps to language development and
to base intervention on the child's currently effective
idiosyncratic system. Practically speaking, the model has
identified mode as a primary component to be assessed and
trained. Unless all effective behaviors are considered in
intervention, training or therapy will continually have to
compete with idiosyncratic and nonlinguistic messages that
will be maintained through strong intermittent reinforcement. Why communicate in a new way (mode) if old ways work?

The second principle of communication theory, that
communication is a function of dyadic feedback, stresses
that any change in one person's communication is dependent
on changes in the other's communication in terms of cues,
consequences, context, and relationship roles. Such a
principle directs the model to include both members of the
child-SO dyad as active clients in remediation. Every
child-SO dyad presents a reciprocal feedback loop in which
the behavior of each person affects and is affected by the
behavior of each other person (Watzlawick, et al., 1967).
Reason does not allow us to expect generalized communicative
change to result from attempts to change the child's behaviors alone if those behaviors were strongly determined and
maintained by their SOs' behaviors in their natural interactions. This conclusion especially applies to those children who have yet to develop a conventional conversation

system that is not yet regularly understood and accepted by strangers.

The third communication principle relating to the current model is that of expectancy or the self-fulfilling prophecy (Bateson, et al., 1956). It is a common clinical event for us to observe parents acting as though they did not expect the child to communicate, or did not know what to expect. In such cases, parents are often rhetorical; they offer few cues or give insufficient time for the child to communicate. This third principle from communication theory states that if a parent treats the child as noncommunicative, then that expectancy may turn into a self-fulfilling prophecy. The child perceives these expectancies and will not communicate. A primary implication of this principle for the model is that a handicapped child's SOs must learn all the ways the child is now sending messages and enter into a consistent relationship with the child that shows acceptance and expectation of the child's communications across contexts. This baseline knowledge of the child's current communicative attempts is essential if the SO is not to extinguish them but to develop them into more conventional forms.

Ecological Theory of Child Development

Recent ecological views of child development and language acquisition (Ainsworth, 1973; Blurton-Jones, 1972; Bronfenbrenner, 1979; Bruner, 1974, 1978b; Lewis and Lee-Painter, 1974; and Mahoney, 1975) converge on one common conclusion: the child and his language develop reciprocally and in tandem with his significant others. Based on years of investigation of early education systems, Bronfenbrenner (1979) argues that studying the child in isolation from his primary dyads ignores the fact that a child and his significant others develop together in a dyad whose joint activities provide the essential context and contingencies for learning.

The thesis that behavior in dyads is generally reciprocal is widely accepted in theory, but is often disregarded in research and clinical practice. The current model translates ecological theory into two operational principles. One, if a child's development is a function inseparable from his significant others, then clinical attention to a delayed

child must extend beyond the delayed child to include therapeutic and educational attention to those significant others
developing with him. Secondly, if a child develops as a
function of his natural learning contexts, then for language
learning to occur, joint activity routines (Bruner, note 2)
and conversational contexts are necessary. Thus, an ecological approach requires the conversational context from
which language emerges (Freedle and Lewis, 1973; Snow, 1978)
and the participation of those significant persons participating in the development of child language. The work of
Ainsworth (1973), Blurton-Jones (1972) and others demonstrate the active role the mother has in the child's development of social skills including language. Ainsworth
concludes that four components of a mother's sensitivity
relate to the child's development of conversation skills: a)
her awareness of the signals, (b) her interpretation of
them, c) an appropriate response to them, and d) a prompt
response to them. The current model places the significant
other in the central role of both dependent (student) and
independent (teacher) variables in a curriculum for initial
communication training.

Pragmatics of Interactive Psycholinguistics

Recent revolutionary changes in views of language
acquisition have resulted in a transition from a focus on
structure (Braine, 1976; Chomsky, 1967) to a focus on the
natural development of language in real life environments
(Bates, 1976; Bloom and Lahey, 1978; Brown, 1978; Bruner,
1975; Moerk, 1972; Nelson, 1980; Snow, 1978;). Such ecological approaches have agreed on several characteristics of
the language development process that may be translated into
the following working principles for an intervention model.
First, language is purposive; that is, it develops from
social, instrumental and personal intentions (Bruner, Roy &
Ratner, 1980; Dore, 1975; Halliday, 1975) involved in sensorimotor development. Thus, the uses of, or reasons for, a
communicative act are as necessary to language development
as are the hitherto dominant form (syntax) and content
(semantics) variables. A corollary implication for intervention is that assessment and training must focus not on
what language or meanings the child has but on what he does
with them. Many handicapped children appear to have little
language when they have more than we expect. But, they are
not conversationally socialized enough to use it very
broadly.

A second principle derived from the pragmatics literature is that language content emerges from prelinguistic
communicative uses. Thus, intervention must consider nonlinguistic communication for its active role as the source
of representational expression and a useful bridge to more
conventional communication. If a language-delayed child's
training involves only linguistic units, it will have stiff
competition from the nonlinguistic communication that often
works well for him, thus, such training will create no need
for advanced linguistic performance in his natural everyday
interactions.

A third principle arising out of pragmatic research is
that language emerges from those primitive parent-child
conversations that exist in the earliest joint activities.
Conversations begin in infancy and are the active source of
the pragmatic (use) and semantic (content) intentions of
language as well as the modelling source of the forms (mode/
form) that are shaped into conventional communication.
Thus, the current model predicts that intervention will
maximize generalization of language to the extent that it
utilizes natural conversations as the locus, process and
goal of language training. Conversation is the essential
reciprocal feedback process which is described by communication theory to be the mechanism responsible for the development of communication behavior (Watzlawick, et al., 1967).
Thus, conversation provides a natural self-perpetuating
training mechanism into which appropriate forms, contents
and uses can be programmed. Conversation is a central
process of the model proposed here. As such, it is both the
central receiver and feedback mechanism for the system in
which communication variables are to be taught.

A fourth principle of pragmatics is that language
develops best when it emerges naturally out of necessity in
real life conversations rather than when taught didactically
as academic units to be stored in memory. Results of
research in pragmatics suggests that natural sensorimotor
and social contingenices will be more successful in building
a generalized language than will rote academic drills isolated from context.

The final principle derived from pragmatic theory is
that language development requires mothers and other SOs to
respond first to the child's behaviors noncontingently until

a communicative repertoire is established, and then to begin to require more conventional performances (uping the ante, Bruner, note 1; or shaping, Skinner, 1953) as the child shows he is able. After observation of over 100 parents of severely language delayed children, we maintain that most of these parents no longer engage in the important upping of the ante or natural shaping. My conclusion is that they often noncontingently accept the child's immature performance and get drawn into the child's idiosyncratic communications, unaware that the child may be training them to communicate at his language level.

Functional Analysis of Behavior

The theoretical and logical perspectives of communication, ecology, and pragmatics provide content and context to the task of language intervention. Within a pragmatic communication ecosystem, we can then look to operant theory (Skinner, 1953; 1957) for engineering principles to be used within the natural teaching conversations. MacCorquodale's (1971) response to Chomsky's critique of Skinner's Verbal Behavior contains a reminder that provides a guideline for applying behavioral principles to natural language development. That reminder is multiple causation, the realization that direct S-R (stimulus-response) relations exist only in stark nongeneralizable events. For the problem of assisted language development, the current model proposes that since communication behavior is a function of personal contingencies and situational contexts, intervention must include spontaneous use of well established training principles such as differential reinforcement, shaping, chaining and various forms of stimulus control. The importance of using these principles spontaneously rather than by predetermined programming is evident in these theories as well as in a careful series of investigations on incidental training effects with conversational preschoolers (Hart and Risley, 1979, 1980; Hart and Rogers-Warren, 1979).

The model proposes that parents and teachers can learn to operate naturally with behavioral contingencies and that the conversational didactic approach is not necessary either for contingent management or language development. Once SOs learn the reciprocal functional nature of their relationship with their child, they can deliberately become strong differential cues and reinforcers for conversational behavior.

General Systems Theory

Interactive events such as communicative transactions have been described by systems theorists as existing within a feedback matrix in which they have reciprocal and cumulative effects on each other. They cannot be adequately explained in isolation (Weinberg, 1975; Bertanfly, 1950). Whether an interaction problem lies in the coordination of telephone transmitters and satellites, or the development of conventional communication between parent and child, systems' principles apply. A primary rule in systems theory is that an adequate analysis of interactive events requires a mapping of components that are logically critical to the prediction and development of such events. These components are seen as repeating within a feedback loop in which they reciprocally and developmentally affect one another.

A major assumption of the current intervention model is that language develops within a communication ecosystem which consists of a series of child communication components, conversation variables and significant other person strategies. The model further assumes that teaching one language component at a time, such as form, content or use, would not be valid in a system which predicts that changing one (e.g. content) also affects the others (e.g. use, mode, conversation). Conversation is viewed as a system whose critical elements can be diagnostically mapped onto an educationally prescriptive format. A major diagnostic and program monitoring strategy in the model is ecomapping. This systems approach to diagnosis illustrates the communicative components for the child and his SO within their conversational context. Treatment is then designed, within the conversation paradigm, to alter all major components interactively and gradually until SOs learn to alter the system as an interactive whole. A prescriptive ecomap can then be drawn as an individualized communication plan (ICP) and verbalized in a training goal statement such as the following: the child will participate in regularly occurring conversations with three turn exchanges; use linguistic modes for action-meanings-content, and instrumental uses; and with his SO chain, wait and model social uses while progressively matching mode, content and use. Such a system's goal is viewed as ecologically more valid than the common unitary goals such as "the child will imitate ten action words." The following discussion presents in detail the components that are proposed for training a communication ecosystem.

Introduction to Taxonomy

The development of the model has involved a process of distilling potentially useful training targets from both the literature and from a series of over one hundred clinical cases. A system of variables was built on the basic structure of three parallel branches: conversation/interaction processes; child communication events; and SO natural teaching strategies. While a formal taxonomy is still evolving, tentative categories have been used to develop experimental tools for assessment and for parent and classroom programming. What is being proposed is a system for professionals to consider when asking, "What should I assess and train if I have a language delayed child who has yet to develop a conventional conversational relationship with strangers?"

Conversation

In the current model, conversation is the locus, process and goal of language intervention. Conversation is defined as a joint activity in which the child and SO exchange messages in a sequence of turns with or without words. Thus, the model proposes a series of interaction behaviors and processes as the central core of events which serve input, feedback, and monitoring functions for the child and SO targets. In other words, interactive events, such as turntaking and chaining, that are required for progressive conversations, are established first with any current child and SO behaviors, regardless of their communicative value. Then, more progressive child and SO behaviors are targeted, but only after SOs establish some form of conversational exchange with the child. Thus, conversation variables are always involved in intervention; in fact, they provide the necessary intentional (social contact reasons) and relational (turntaking and chaining) structure within which child language and SO strategies will be fostered.

The unique value of the response classes in the conversation taxonomy is that they force the issue that language training is for communication, and must involve the child and his SOs in tandem. A close corollary is that the conversational episode is the most appropriate vehicle for the natural teaching and learning of the child's language modes, meanings, and uses.

The relational nature of interactional events created such problems of clarity that operational definitions were posed in order to build a structure of conversation that could be observed with reasonable reliability and necessary social validity. Current approaches to discourse analysis (Coulthard, 1977; Mishler, 1978; Widdowson, 1974), and second language learning (Van Ek, 1977; Wilkins, 1972, 1974) provided some conceptual help, but their exclusive attention to linguistic semantics and structure precluded any but a conceptual application to the task of teaching individuals with no linguistic performance.

Thus, the problem has been to select response classes for the development of conversations that may or may not involve words or any other conventional structure. Recent studies of language within joint action routines between mother and infants provided concrete directions for a taxonomy of conversational variables (Bruner, note 2; Freedle and Lewis, 1973; Snow and Ferguson, 1978; Stern, 1974). Additionally, our own work with handicapped children in parent and teacher contexts led us to a series of analyses of conversations.

The series of targets under the model's conversation structure includes the following: social recognition events, purposive social contacts, joint activities, turn-taking, chains, initiations, responses, topic initiations, shifts, closes, and off-topic behavior, all of which can be executed with or without words. In fact, a pervasive thrust of the model is to teach SOs that a persistent nonlinguistic conversation system is necessary before generalized productive language will emerge and that the nonlinguistic system may be useful as a retreat when linguistic demand is too great.

Social Recognition. The first set of targets for conversation building are those targets that show sufficient social recognition for productive contacts. Some handicapped children, such as the "autistic-like," act as though they notice little of what others do. Experienced families and professionals know that many of these children show

later in their language that they had been very socially
attentive to the situations. It is essential for SOs to
identify and train increased signaling of social awareness
in their child, both in initiations and responses. Once an
SO notices the child recognizing or responding to her, she
can seize upon that event as an opportunity for a brief
conversation. For example, if the sensitive mother sees the
child's eyes following her to the door, she can try to make
it a conversation by extending her arms or saying "Wanna
come?" and then taking turns with any response the child
makes.

Social Contact Purposes (SCP). Our clinical observations of handicapped children with their parents and
teachers repeatedly reveal that the adult seizes on few of
the many natural opportunities for conversation that exist
in their interactions. The interaction category of SCP has
been identified as a principle device for generating conversations. Under the rationale that language and communication develop within nonlinguistic and linguistic interactions (Bruner, note 2; Lewis, 1972; Stern, Jaffee, Beebe &
Bennett, 1975) a primary goal of the model is to increase
the range and depth of conversationally contingent interactions. Units for interaction episodes may be discovered
parallel to the way the pragmatic language revolution found
its units, by responding to the question, "what is the
communicative act apparently intended to do?" (Dore, 1975;
Searle, 1969). Similarly, we ask of parent-child interactions, why is the event initiated? In other words, a
social contact purpose is the pragmatic intent of the
initiation of an interaction with another.

The primary function of SCPs is to assess and prescribe
interactions and to prepare the child for a wide range of
natural communication situations. Interaction pragmatics
(i.e. purposes-uses-reasons-intentions-desired effects) give
rise to a variety of communication pragmatics (examples to
be supplied). Why teach mode, content, and use if there
doesn't exist the range of social contacts that will allow
these communicative components to emerge and generalize?

When we have the child and SOs range of SCPs, we can
then logically deduct and clinically predict situations for
the dual purpose of prescribing for their own developmental
value as well as for their use as the loci for training.

.

Each SCP has the potential for initiating an interaction episode. The model views every SCP as an "opportunity for conversation". Too often these contacts, if noticed at all, are ended perfunctorily. It is our intent to develop an intermittent program of SCPs that will establish conversations with sufficient breadth to span an increasing range of topics and uses. Both active and potential SCPs are targets in the model. "Active" SCPs are natural events or behaviors that could easily be turned into a conversation.

Joint Activity Routines. Once a social contact is extended into a conversation, the question often is, now what? The better the SO understands the child's perceptual, motivational and sensorimotor world, the easier it will be to develop joint activity routines that can be used to get many conversations going. The joint activity or play ritual is a central mechanism in the model. In fact, a primary assessment strategy is to record scripts of a range of common joint activities, then analyze the events into a communication ecosystem that displays the current child and SO events.

Such a routine ecosystem analysis is useful for individualized educational planning as well as prescriptive programming and monitoring. Clinical observations often reveal that handicapped children engage in few extended joint activity routines. These essential sources of natural language learning must be modeled and prescribed as the foundation of all language development. We start with social contact for the purpose of entering the child's world exactly where he is, treating his behaviors as communicative, then showing him that the SO will either upset the routine or wait and cue him to communicate. In assessment and training, the social interaction patterns between the child and SO are considered. If the pattern is a didactic one in which the SO and child are in a question-answer and SO controlled relation, natural conversational learning of the language targets will be limited. If the relation is associative or cooperative, the implicit rules will allow following the other's lead and sharing the balance of power, thus offering more opportunities for generalized learning.

One strategy utilized in the model is to increase gradually the social and contingent nature of the interaction, in order that the handicapped child is taught that he can develop conversation from activities of his choosing. Operationally, this increased socialization of joint activity is attempted along somewhat the following lines; solo to parallel to associative to cooperative to social-didactic to social-caretaking. The SO observes the child playing alone (solo) noting his motivations, skills, and problems sufficiently to be able to then play beside the child (parallel) with materials and in ways similar to the child's performance, thus setting the stage for modeling. During parallel play, the SO will make her activity vivid and interesting with the double intention of modeling ways to communicate about the activity and bringing the child into her activity. Whether the child does or does not join in, the SO will now begin to play with him associatively performing a little above the child's levels for effective modeling and establishing a conversation by initiating, waiting, responding, signaling turns, and chaining. During associative play, there are neither goals to reach nor formal contingencies to establish. Next, after the SO is well received in the activity and is an accepted source of reward, the SO can turn the activity into one in which there is a goal that requires both partners share responsibility and exchange information to achieve the goal (cooperative). In cooperative play, more formal contingencies such as upping the ante and differential attention, may be most successful. After the child's relations with the SO have been well established in solo to cooperative patterns, conversation skills can be established in caretaking and didactic relations. The danger of caretaking and didactic relations as sources for language training is that they often become one-sided and lose the balanced content, activity, and purpose of good natural learning situations (Bronfenbrenner, 1979; Nelson, 1979; Bruner, note 1). Such activities often have external contingencies for the adult that limit their value as conversations.

Turntaking and Chaining. Once a conversation begins, what is structurally necessary for its maintenance? Beyond shared topic and sufficient match of communicative modes, turntaking and chaining are two essential tools for any conversation. These two relational processes are necessary for messages to proceed without interruption and with some meaningful relation to each other. Turntaking requires that only one member in a dyad sends a message at a time and that there is a hierarchy of ways to signal another to take or

yield his turn. To the extent that a turn is a communicative message, it can occur in any or all modes. SOs are
instructed to attend carefully to the child's behavior as
potential turns in a conversation. They learn to treat all
productive child behavior as communicative, as turns in a
potential primitive conversation. A primary goal in training is to extend the turntaking length (TTL) of conversation
across appropriate social contact purposes. Just as MLU is
a reflection of increasing linguistic competence (Brown,
1973), TTL may well become an index of communicative competence (Sacks, Schegloff & Jefferson, 1974; Schegloff,
1973). The turn is similar to Sinclair and Caulthard's
(1975) move which is their basic unit in discourse analysis.
SOs are trained to keep the child in increasingly longer
turns, thus exposing the child attentively to increasing
language and general learning models.

The second relational tool, chaining, is more complex
than turntaking. A communicative chain which is an adapta-
tion of the Skinnerian principle (Skinner, 1953) is a message that is both a response to the other person's message
and a cue for the partner to communicate again. Observation
of many child-SO dyads reveals that the partners often
respond in a dead-end manner that stops the conversation.
The chain is a particularly flexible tool for natural language training in that all the SO needs to remember is to
respond increasingly to the child in a way that keeps him in
the interaction. As with turntaking, no behavioral level or
communicative mode is exempt from chaining. When training
professionals and parents to chain their messages with the
child's into conversations, we find that if they stop and
think how they should chain, the process is thwarted. When
the same SOs attend carefully to the child's current activities and to the logical flow of the joint activity, the
problem of how and what to chain is solved by the general
dictum: keep him in there.

Turn balance and turn dominance are two corollary
targets for training. SOs are trained to approach a reasonable share of turns with the child so that neither dominates
the communication. SOs learn to follow the child's behavioral lead and to wait for the child to take a turn, thus
teaching him the basic communication rule that you must give
in order to get in the conventional world of interactions.
In the experimental parent program, it is not uncommon to

see ratios of 5-1 and even 12-1 in favor of the SOs turns. Parents report that such turn dominance is what they do in response to the recommendation "talk to your child." Perhaps "take turns with your child" will prove to be a more language productive recommendation.

Once interactive turntaking within shared activities is a natural part of the child's relations with his significant others, the issue arises as to what specific language and communicative skills are to be taught. The following sections present first the communicative components for child and SO, then the system of natural teaching strategies for SOs. Those child and SO target areas are presented as the content to be programmed into a conversational structure. The discussions to follow must be taken as descriptions of what to test and train within natural conversations.

Child Components of Model

Attention both to delayed children and to recent findings in child language studies results in an acute awareness that language can be understood only if its form, content and function or use (Bloom and Lahey, 1978) are independently considered. Our observations of hundreds of delayed children reveal that some are most notably delayed in linguistic form or physical mode, while others show greater delays in cognitive content or pragmatic mode, while others show greater delays in cognitive content or pragmatic uses. Thus, a "language problem" is a meaningless or ambiguous label at best. Until adequate assessment of the child's modes (and collorary forms), content (meanings) and uses (intentions) becomes a regular part of intervention, professionals will continue to diagnose and prescribe for the child on the basis of their own definition of language (usually in terms of linguistic content and syntax).

The taxonomy proposed for child components in the model is an attempt to set forth a pool of communicative classes (mode, content and use) that develop on a continuum from nonlinguistic or body language, through vocalizations up into linguistic expressions. Every communicative act whether intentional or unintentional has a mode, content and use and can be expressed nonlinguistically, vocally, linguistically or in combinations thereof. Thus, if language is to be taught for its communicative function, the model proposes that language be assessed and trained within the communicative structure (mode, content and use) and along the developmental continuum beginning in nonlinguistic communications from which language emerges naturally. (Bloom and Lahey, 1978; Bruner, 1974; Snow, 1972).

Mode

Little direct familiarity with developmentally delayed children is needed to realize that language in its conventional sense is at times an unrealistic immediate goal for many of these children who usually communicate quite effectively with idiosyncratic performance understandable only to familiar persons. If we simply shift our primary concern from language to communication, then we bring into our professional domain populations of children who have been excluded from or mistargeted in training because that training was linguistically based.

A common set of conclusions in over two hundred diagnostic evaluations of these children has been: first, the child's language (i.e. conventional symbolic referential system) is severely delayed for his age. But, then we find ourselves making a perplexing third conclusion: the child's current communication system is working quite well for him. This third conclusion rests on the child's successful idiosyncratic communication with those persons who have finely-tuned themselves to the child's particular code. Thus, in order to identify primary targets for language training, we must accept that language content and structure comes in large measure from communication, and that we must look first to the question: How is a child communicating?

In our work developing a model for communication intervention, a major breakthrough came when our basic target moved from language to communication. Working with parents, teachers and students to operate from this perspective has illustrated how deeply ingrained is the "speech" or verbal bias to our work with handicapped children. Once these individuals have learned to differentially attend to the child's modes of communication, they come into a closer more fruitful match with the child. Only minimal direct contact with these children is needed to realize how powerful a competitor the child's nonlinguistic and vocal communication is to his struggling linguistic communication that is emerging.

By including all modes of communication into language intervention, the model is targeting three goals. The first is to insure that intervention begins at a child's current stage of communicative development under the premise that the child's language competence develops along a continuum of his communicative competence. The second purpose for including mode as a formal component is to encourage professionals and parents to enroll in intervention any language-delayed child regardless of his modes of communication. If communication is accepted as the vehicle for language development, then a communication model applies to all delayed individuals, and no child is "not ready for therapy." A third use of the mode component is as a way to discover the child's prelinguistic semantics (meanings) and pragmatics (uses). Clearly, the child has linguistic meanings and pragmatic intentions long before he begins talking. Unless we seriously consider all the child's communicative modes, a linguistic approach will miss much of the child's semantic and pragmatic communicative competence. In addition, attention to all modes will provide a more valid vehicle for exploring the child's cognitive competence than will linguistically based assessment approaches.

Recent research in the pragmatics of language (Austin, 1962; Bates, 1976; Dore, 1975), communication theory (Watzlawick et al., 1967) parent-child interaction (Lewis and Rosenblum, 1974) and sociolinguistics (Ervin-Tripp, 1978; and Hymes, 1972 a and b) alerts us to the importance of investigating the variety of modes in which language develops.

The concept of mode is similar to Hymes' (1972b) channel which is a component of speech that differentiates the oral from the written, televised, and so on. Hymes also has been especially helpful in broadening the goal in linguistic theory from the description of the speaker's linguistic competence to a concern with communicative competence, which extends beyond traditional linguistic modes or channels. The inclusion of mode as a basic component to the current model allows us to include in our target classes all the child's behaviors that effectively communicate and to set as a goal the sending of appropriate messages (Hymes, 1977).

Communicative functions of language first begin when SOs interpret a child's random behaviors as though they had

communicative intentions (perlocutionary). Thus, any behaviors may become communicative if they regularly have communicative effects. The utility of the perlocutionary
concept for intervention is that it opens the child's total
behavioral repertoire as a potential source for the basic
units for language development. The perlocutionary concept
also focuses on the primary role the SO has in determining
which behaviors may become communicative. If SOs expect the
child not to communicate, they may miss many natural opportunities to treat the child's initially random behaviors as
communicative in such a way that the child will never
develop intentional communicative messages.

The illocutionary stage follows in which the child
begins to send messages intentionally. Here SOs must become
sensitized to the full range of language the child will use.
Often SOs appear to take for granted (i.e., fail to contingently respond to) natural signals and movements that need
immediate response for maintainance and development into the
locutionary stage, in which the child uses conventional
signs and symbols to communicate. At any stage of development the child will perform perlocutionary and illocutionary
acts in novel situations or with novel content. Adults, in
fact, are observed to operate at both perlocutionary and
illocutionary levels when confronted with a foreign lanuage
(Van Ek, 1977). At a train station in Brussels, for example, where no one language is dominant, a traveler's expressions and movements, while not intended to communicate, in
fact will have sent a message to all observers regardless of
native language. Then, with his second language dictionary
he will perform at the locutionary level when time and skill
permits. Similarly many language delayed children must be
seen as potentially communicating all three levels at any
stage independently.

Certainly, some severely handicapped individuals are
limited mainly to perlocutionary or illocutionary communication but careful attention also must be paid to two separate
communication systems that too often are professionally
ignored. These are idiosyncratic and conventional systems.
Operationally, a child's conventional communication system
includes those modes, contents and uses that are understood
and accepted by his significant others. All perlocutionary,
illocutionary and locutionary behaviors are included.

Logic as well as clinical observations of over 200 children with parents or teachers argue strongly that SOs "see" and respond to a greater range of child behaviors as communicative than do professionals or strangers. While this observation may seem intuitive, this idosyncratic-conventional distinction is seldom systematically considered in assessing and determining educational and therapeutic placement. The importance of the idiosyncratic-conventional distinction lies in the fact that a child's communicative competence can be known fully only by discovering those communicative modes, contents and uses that are having communicative effects in his idiosyncratic relations with familiar others. Anyone experienced with cerebral palsied children, for example, will not be surprised by the notion of idiosyncratic communication, especially if they know parents who have developed elaborate codes for translating their child's complex body movements into predictable meanings. No stranger would know this communicative system without intense experience.

The model recommends that SOs and professionals assume that all behavior, regardless of mode, can communicate, and that they apply a "stranger test" in their natural teaching intervention with the child. With the "stranger test" a person asks himself when communicating with a child, "would a stranger understand and accept this child's communication?" and, if not, "what can I do to our interactions to make him more communicative with me right now?" The strong influence of idiosyncratic communications as a competitor with the struggling and emerging conventional performance is perhaps the most compelling argument for considering the modes of communication as basic to any ecologically valid approach to language intervention. In other words, how can more mature and conventional communication emerge when the child's current idiosyncratic communication is maintained by regular intermittent understanding and is thus reinforced?

The content and sequence of classes of communicative modes in the model is a product of three processes; first, clinical judgments of the modes used by over 100 developmentally delayed children from ages 1 to 8 years, with diagnoses of autism, mild to severe retardation, cerebral palsy, severe emotional disturbance, deafness, and aphasia; second, a survey of research on the forms of early communication performance (Bates, 1974; Dunst, 1978; Ferguson, 1975; Mayo,

1979; Moore and Meltzoff, 1978; Oller, 1978; and Seibert, 1980), and third, analyses of performance of 18 normally-developing children videotaped in interactions with their mothers.

The major classes of nonlinguistic, vocal and linguistic behaviors are distinguished first on the pragmatic basis that natural use requires that parents and teachers need a few simple distinctions they can observe and remember for natural training. For clarity, the nonlinguistic set of modes is characterized as communications "without words," the vocal set as communications " with sounds," and the linguistic set as communications "with words." A fourth set of modes, a model mix, is necessary to account for the obvious and desired use of multiple modes. The major question the SO learns to ask is: "what mode is affecting me as communicative?" The model educates SOs to learn the child's current modes, their own current responses to them and the changes needed to build more progressive modes.

As seen in Table 1 the interaction between Chris (C) and her mother (M) in the above script illustrates the variety of communicative modes both in terms of their physical form (NL, V, L) and communicative intentions (P, I, L). In the first turn, C is apparently engaged in sound play which shows no communicative intention. However, M interprets C's vocalizations as a communication. Thus, C's performance can be coded as a vocal, perlocutionary act and M's turn 2 performance as linguistic in mode, locutionary in intention. Notice that the mother first accepts any behavior as communicative and then builds a chained conversation that requires increasingly more advanced communicative modes.

Child Communicative Content

The second component of a child's communication system in the model is the semantic or referential feature, in other words, the content of messages. The content component is the answer to the question: What in his world is the child communicating about? A common observation and home report is that the delayed child knows much more than he communicates. Another observation is that programs often teach languge units that are of questionable if any communicative value to the child. The "color, shape and size" habit of teaching often precedes the child's communication of his basic experiences and intentions.

Table 1

MODE
ILLUSTRATIONS
SCRIPT EXAMPLES

			Mode			Intention		
	Turns		NL	V	L	P	I	L
1.	C	LYING IN BED "BA BA BA BA BA"	x			x		
2.	M	"want bottle?"			x			x
3.	M	"no, time to get out"			x			x
4.	C	REACHES TO M, "0, 0, 0"		x				x
5.	M	waits with arms extended, quizzical look	x				x	
6.	C	"OUT"			x			x
7.	M	"huh?"		x			x	
8.	C	"WANT OUT, MA"			x			x
9.	M	"I want out, okay,"			x			x
10.	M	"here we go." lifts child			x			x

Key: NL-Nonlinguistic   P=Perlocutionary
     V-Vocal   I=Illocutionary
     L-Linguistic   L=Locutionary

The current model takes a pragmatic or communicative approach toward selecting the content classes for training. Such an approach first identifies the range of meanings that the child currently communicates in either nonlinguistic, vocal or linguistic modes; these meanings are then taken as the baseline from which to select the next content goals that would add most to his current communication skills. For easy translation to SOs, three vocabularies are identified: nonlinguistic, vocal and linguistic, to represent the child's meanings communicated without words, with sounds, and with words, respectively. For a child who communicates frequently, but only nonlinguistically, the goal for the SO may be to "second-language train" those nonlinguistic messages into vocal or linguistic productions, that is, to teach the child sounds or words that would appropriately translate the messages into a more conventional production. Needless to say, the ideal time for such training will be at the moment the child sends a message and is motivated to attend to the word and tolerate contingencies requiring it. Thus, SOs learn to translate the child's nonlinguistic communications to words that would be acceptable verbal messages for the given context.

This nonlinguistic vocabulary would then comprise those meanings that the child now cares to communicate about and that would be initial targets in first linguistic training. The child's own current communication, even if at signal or gestural level, is the most sound response to the question: "What do we teach the child to communicate?"

For another child, the goal may be to develop horizontally a broader vocabulary base for conversation building (rather than the vertical second-language-training task). As a primary strategy for vocabulary building the model proposes that a sample of the child's common social contact purposes (e.g, to help, to give information, to play, etc.) be identified, then functional scripts be written, identifying what new meanings will most efficiently allow the child to build conversations in those situations. This approach is another pragmatic attack on the language content learning problem; vocabulary targets are selected first from the child's current conversations and then from those common social episodes in which the child develops.

The formal content classes in the model's taxonomy are social contact topics and semantic referent classes. After review of several works studying child communicative topics (Brown, 1973; Clark, 1973; MacNamara, 1972), no classification appeared that lent itself directly to a communicative approach to semantic development. Consequently, a search was made of the topics initiated between normal and severely delayed children (from minimal communication to broad use of three word sentences) and their parents and/or teachers (MacDonald, 1978). A recurrent finding was that the topics of conversation could be discriminated in terms of the social contact purposes--the pragmatic intention of the contact. Such intentions as "getting help," "nurturing," "playing," and "getting information" gave the SOs ripe opportunities to develop those contacts into conversations. A primary training goal is to create and seize upon natural social contact purposes; and then to keep the child interacting for increasingly longer turns as new vocabulary units are modeled and shaped appropriately for the social context.

The SOs are trained to discover the child's current vocabularies, the one without words and the one with words, so they can both second-language train and build conversations. For specific words, the model goes to the now well established literature on the development of semantic relations in early verbal language (Bloom and Lahey, 1978; Brown, 1973; MacDonald and Blott, 1974; MacDonald, 1978; Schlesinger, 1971; Streml and Waryas, 1974). The broadly based studies agree across several languages and cultures that a few semantic or meaning classes account for a majority of the words in children's first sentences. These classes include agent, action, object, location and experience in particular, and of later importance, modification, introduction, possession, and recurrence (MacDonald, 1978). These classes have been utilized successfully in an assessment inventory (MacDonald, 1978), a teaching series (Horstmeier and MacDonald, 1978), and in programs for total communication (Lombardino, Willems and MacDonald, 1981) and in the current model in an attempt to apply them systematically to use in conversations. The earlier programs were more directly language oriented and considered for linguistic communication exclusively. In the current model, the same semantic classes are seem as cognitively descriptive of early nonlinguistic communications as well.

As seen in Table 2, Script A illustrates the second language training strategy which respects the clear or potential semantic intentions of all the child's communications by translating each into a more conventional production that the child may some day use in similar situations (turns 3, 6, 8 and 10). Notice in the contrasting Script B that the mother misses all four opportunities to treat her child's behavior as communicative (i.e. illocutionary) and to naturally teach the child a more conventional way to communicate in similar future settings.

Table 2

CONTENT

Content Script A			Content Script B		
Turns			**Turns**		
1.	M	"let's go"	M	"let's go"	
2.	C	SHAKES HEAD	C	SHAKES HEAD	
3.	M	"no?"	M	"oh, yes you will"	
4.	M	picks C up	M	picks child up	
5.	C	WAVES TO OTHER CHILD	C	WAVES TO CHILD	
6.	M	"bye bye," leaves room	M	"let's go"	
7.	C	"KA KA"	C	"KA KA"	
8.	M	"car, go in car"	M	"I have to stop at the store"	
9.	C	"DADDY"	C	"DADDY"	
10.	M	"gonna see daddy"	M	"we need bread and milk"	

Use

The discussions on mode and content are responses to the traditional questions in child language study and intervention: "How is the child communicating?" and "What is he communicating?" Once the pivotal focus shifts from language structure to communicative use, as the present model prescribes, the question "Why is the child communicating?" becomes primary. This question leads to critical programming decisions--especially if it is found that the child's communications are limited to basic needs. Such a "crisis language" affords few of the natural opportunities for conversation that declarations, requests, replies and other communicative acts offer.

Recent years have seen a "pragmatics" revolution in child language study as well as in general linguistics (Coulthard, 1977; Sacks, et al., 1974) and sociolinguistics

(Ervin-Tripp, 1978; and Hymes, 1972b). This revolution has viewed language as developing within a communicative context and for social reasons such as to get information, declare, inform, reply, protest. After years of direct contact with autistic, retarded, cerebral palsied, deaf and language delayed children, I am struck by two major pragmatic problems. First, the children communicate for only a few reasons and act as though they don't know what to do with the language meanings and communicative skills they do have. Second, their SOs are frequently rhetorical rather than conversational; that is, they do not communicate for a response (Watzlawick, et al., 1967).

The role of the child's SOs in this task is critical in that they are in a unique position to give the child reasons to communicate. Often, we see handicapped children who rarely have reason to communicate beyond basic needs or crises. Their SOs often anticipate their communications and provide fewer contingencies and expectancies for broader social uses of communication. The nature of the child and SO's relationship will also determine the child's range of pragmatics; children in primarily caretaking or didactic relations may have few reasons to communicate other than to demand and protest. Along the same continuum of relations, if the SO and child have a playful, joint action relationship, they will make mini-conversations out of almost any contact and in these conversations SOs can model and encourage the range of uses the child needs if he is to learn to play a variety of communicative roles with others.

The initial question to ask in a pragmatic analysis of communication is: "To what extent are the child and the SO's behaviors communicating?" Immediately, the issue of intention versus effect arises. Should we look at the intentions or the effects of the child's communication? The perplexing answer must be yes--both. The model attempts to teach SOs to shape more of the child's behaviors that currently do not appear to be intended for communication. If the earliest communicative behaviors emerge from those random infant movements contingently responded to by the mother (Bruner, 1974; Freedle and Lewis, 1977; Lewis, 1972; Nelson, 1979; Stern, 1977), then a fitting clinical strategy may be to treat any of the delayed child's behaviors as anticipatory of the response. Then, by definition, the child will be communicating intentionally.

The pragmatic approach is useful also in that it offers a series of categories that are programmed parallel to the mode and content targets. As with mode and content, communicative use begins as soon as communication begins. Thus, no child is at too low a level for pragmatic development, and no delayed child is too young for communication training. The taxonomy for use has developed out of three sources: extensive review of early pragmatic development (particularly, Bates, 1976; Bruner, 1975; Dore, 1975; Moerk, 1977; Searle, 1969; Wells, 1974), a series of studies with delayed and non-delayed children and their mothers (Almerico and MacDonald, 1979; Lombardino, 1978; Owens, 1978) and twenty parent-based language training programs.

The taxonomy was developed with and for a population of children judged to be communicating much less than they know. This target population displays severe delay in the frequency and complexity of linguistic and nonlingusitic conversations. The children seldom respond to others' communications immediately and regularly fail to initiate communications when their best developmental interest will benefit. Further, they generally do not see that their actions can be used communicatively to build relationships. Consequently, several revisions of our classification of pragmatic acts have resulted in a taxonomy that reflects both developmental research on mother-child interaction (Dore, 1975; Lombardino, 1978; Owens, 1978; Wells, 1974) and careful clinical surveys of communication problems exhibited by developmentally delayed children. The taxonomy is designed for parallel description of the child's and the SO's uses. Given the model's underlying assumption that SOs are in an ubiquitous language training relationship with the child, the parallel taxonomy allows for analysis of appropriate match and potential modeling effects.

Three major categories, personal, social and instrumental, were derived from the mass of category systems developed for children of varying developmental levels (Bruner, 1975; Dore, 1975; Searle, 1969; Wells, 1974). The personal uses include each of those behaviors whose primary purpose is to express the self rather than to communicate with others. The motivation of a personal act comes from the child with no apparent intention to get something (instrumental) or to contact others (social); for example, the child may cry when he falls but not for attention or help. While observation of the context reveals that the personal message has no apparent communicative purpose, the model proposes that personal acts may acquire communicative purpose, the model proposes that personal acts may acquire communicative purpose naturally if they have systematic effects (e.g, getting attention or getting help). For example, the child who cries as he falls may then get mom's attention; later he may cry intentionally to get her attention. Thus personal uses can be powerful perlocutionary bases for natural communication training. The personal use category also allows for attention to the sensorimotor stages of development, in which the child's "egocentric" communication (Piaget, 1971) may dominate for functions such as practicing, accompanying action, and pretending. These personal functions may offer SOs ways to gradually get into the child's world by matching the child's communicative functions to establish an effective model for later shaping to more social or instrumental functions.

The "instrumental" category of uses includes communications by which the child either effectively or intentionally gets something or manipulates others to do something. A common obstacle to the language development of delayed children arises in the child's increasing physical independence and decreasing need to communicate with others. The communications of handicapped children I have observed are often primarily instrumental and limited to crisis situations. Otherwise, the child's usual independent functioning allows him to proceed without communicating. In the model, SOs design life situations in order to maximize the child's need to communicate. Also, instrumental uses are recommended as places to begin advanced mode and content training. For example, a motivated child who already requests help might be trained to do so using higher modes or new content, thus, capitalizing on an old use (request) to develop new modes or contents.

The third category in the taxonomy is "social." Here the primary purpose for communication is to get, maintain or respond to social contact. "Social" communications place emphasis on conversational interaction. In social communication acts, the other person appears to be important to the child for the person himself and not only for the purpose of serving the child's extrasocial needs (instrumental) or his egocentric status (personal). It is the social uses of

language that need developmental attention if the child is
to establish those conversational relations with others that
are necessary for language development. Social uses are
much more available as opportunities to communicate once the
child sees, through natural conditioning, attachment or
both, that social contact and attention in themselves are
communication goals.

The child's SOs must learn that adquate language learning will come only if the child has a pool of pragmatic
tools for staying in conversations, for it is these conversations that are critical for language development. To
conclude, the present system views a child's current communicative uses first as the basis for training more mature
model production and new content. The model then proposes
to extend the child's communicative uses beyond his basic
needs to uses that establish necessary social and learning
exchanges. As a general goal, the pragmatic targets are
tools for moving the child out of his egocentric world to
more reciprocal social experiences. The question now becomes an interactive one of "what to teach the SOs to do in
their interactions with the child in order to facilitate
language within conversational relations. A series of
strategies and concerns will be discussed in detail, given
that the role of SOs is usually taken for granted as competent by virtue of adult status. In the current model, the
SO plays as critical a client role as does the child.

Significant Other (SO) Variables

In the current model, the delayed child's parents,
teachers and other significant persons play as important a
role in the child's language development as does the child
himself. The model proposes that improved child communication requires that his significant others come to play
active roles as students, clients, teachers and environmental engineers of their home or classroom.

Playing the role of student is necessary in order for
SOs to learn the essential components of a communication
system and to become aware of their child's current performance profile in that system. Such observational knowledge
enables the SO to model appropriately and to relate contingently with the child in ways that have natural teaching
effects. The role of client is required under the rationale

that a child's communication develops within primary dyads (Bronfenbrenner, 1979) involving the child and his SOs; thus, changes in both members of the dyads are necessary in order for communication to develop optimally. A taxonomy of potential teaching variables has evolved in the model from developmental literature (particularly, interactive psycholinguistics, behavioral and modeling paradigms, communication theory and ecological views of child development) and several years of clinical programming with parents and teachers. The taxonomy is an initial attempt to juxtapose clinical and curricular targets for the SOs against the taxonomy for the child clients.

Following the acquisition of observational knowledge about her child, the SO is to map her own communication performance with the child. Given the natural influences of modeling (Bandura, 1977), referencing (Bruner, note 1), contingent responding (Nelson, 1980), behaviorism, (Skinner, 1953); and didactic learning (Hunt, 1961) it is logical to consider the SO's language and communication performance as having a reciprocally dynamic influence on the physical (mode), cognitive (form and content), pragamatic (use) and conversational development of child's communication. Thus, SOs learn that their spontaneous ways of communicating may be redesigned for maximal natural training value.

Changes in SO communication result in inadvertent teaching effects. But the SO also must play a more deliberate role first as teacher, then, to the point of habituating those principles that establish a progressive communicative relationship with the child. Two series of strategies are proposed: one directed to training the language components of mode, content and use, and another directed toward conversation training. The separation of SO strategies into distinct classes involves considerable overlap, but is useful if we are to differentially diagnose the SO's knowledge and skills in nurturing the complexities of communication.

Just as the SO's communication and natural teaching skills affect the child's language development, so also do their expectations, although in a less apparent way. Their expectations of the child can frequently become a behaviorally effective self-fulfilling prophecy (Bateson, et al., 1966; Watzlawick, 1967). Many parents behave as though they do not expect the child to communicate at all or any more maturely. Parents and teachers who talk for the child or who are regularly rhetorical can be behaviorally interpreted as teaching the child to communicate neither more nor differently. The model attempts to establish expectancy as a directly observable series of events to evaluate and train.

The entire taxonomy of SO variables is seen as a parallel and integrative part of the child's total communication ecosystem. These variables are seen as both independent and dependent, interchangeable in their functional role in a communication program. In order to develop spontaneous communication, the child needs to operate within primary dyads that involve reciprocal and cooperative relations that up the ante as he develops, and that yield the balance of power to the child as appropriate. The current model proposes a series of variables that allow the SO to productively perform the roles of student, client, teacher and environmental engineer.

Active Observational Knowledge

If SOs are to stimulate progressive language in the child naturally, they must first know two things about his communication system. First, they must have a gross developmental scheme of a child's communication system; and second, they need a map of their child's current behavioral placement in that system. An example may illustrate a typical knowledge problem that we have had to resolve before any child-matched language and communication training could proceed systematically. Parents and teachers are often anxious to train expressive language in a child before he has the conversation skills basic to natural language learning. They engage in word training with little attention to the child's current communication system; i.e., with little attention to its nonlinguistic modes, contents, uses and conversational aspects. Thus, these well-intentioned teachers attempt to train language independently of the child's current communication system, instead of realizing that this system forms the necessary base for training more advanced communication and acts as a formidable competitor to new communication. Such is the case especially if the child's current idiosyncratic system is being maintained by adults who accept, understand and reinforce it.

A fundamental premise of the model is that during all of his communicative interactions a child is constantly and naturally taught not only how (mode), what (content-semantics), and why (use-pragmatics) to communicate, but also how to be conversational. Language learning is not primarily an academic task; it is a natural conversational process that engages the child's physical (mode), cognitive (content) and social pragmatic (use and conversation) skills simultaneously. A logical corrolary to this premise of ubiquitous training is that those natural trainers (SOs) must learn to see the child in a communication ecosystem in order that they may come to interact naturally with the child, through contingent modeling that progressively models and differentially shapes more mature performance.

Thus, an ecologically valid curriculum and a natural training relationship (the first ideally leads to the second) would include training directed to teaching SOs the essential components of a communicative ecosystem, their child's current performance profile or map in that system, and the next steps for progressive development or lateral generalization. We are currently constructing a curriculum for professionals along this line to prepare them to manage parent and classroom programs. The task is not as difficult as it may appear to students who have struggled to learn new language systems. Parents and other persons untrained in language and communication can easily see the child's linguistic and nonlinguistic communications in terms of how (mode), what (content) and why (use) the child communicates. They need only a little more evidence from their own child's interactions to see the crucial but ignored, conversations (with and without words) that dominate his life.

SOs do not need to learn all the discriminations within the taxonomy. They do, however, need to learn to identify a general pattern of the child's system, for example, they might notice that the child communicates primarily with mime movements and non-speech sounds (mode) about his own actions (content) mainly for reasons of crisis such as demand and command (use), and that he stays for as many as six turns in nonlinguistic conversations if physical interaction is involved (conversation). The family or school personnel of such a child would learn to observe _when_ these various communication components occur, _what_ the next logical targets would be and _how_ to foster these components within this conversational relationship with the child.

Before that discussion, a comment on observational knowledge per se. One observation reported by several professionals who have trained teachers and parents has been that the adults appear to change their interactions with the child as a function of learning the critical elements of the child's communication. That is, when a parent or teacher comes to observe the child differently, her expectations and contingencies with him change accordingly. A conceptual mnemonic device is often suggested once the SOs know what to observe. It is the "lonely island test." Using this strategy, the SO imagines being isolated with the child on an island and being dependent on that child for all the natural rewards of communication. Then, with the child's current communicative map in hand (in mind eventually), the SO asks herself, "What changes would I want in the child's communication in order to make me less lonely." The answers then become targets that are important enough to the SOs that they will be willing to change their interactions in order to reach those targets. By observing developmentally appropriate and inappropriate targets, SOs come to attend differentially to the child's emerging communications, thereby reaching the first step in becoming a natural communication teacher. Thus, the goal of this first series of components is to establish the SO as a competent student of the child's communicative ecosystem. The model specifies that a child's SOs must be students of his communication before they can become more effective natural teachers.

General Teaching Principles for Significant Others

A hierarchy of natural teaching principles has evolved through the application of the various theoretical and research resources discussed earlier to clinical and experimental use with the model in a series of parent and classroom programs. It became apparent that targeting specific strategies was not sufficient to establish SOs as progressive language teachers within conversations. Consequently, a series of theoretically diverse and operationally defined principles are now used in training SOs to assume a new more communicatively fruitful role with the child. These principles are applied throughout the training sequences as they apply to targets for various components.

1.   The ubiquity principle derives from the consistent clinical conclusion and from the premise in communica-

tion theory that <u>all behavior communicates</u> and thus, you cannot <u>not</u> communicate. A corollary, grounded in behavioral principles, is that if all behaviors have communicative effects, then, they also have natural teaching effects since any communication provides contingent feedback and cues to the child's immediate behavior. Thus, the very act of communicating with a child is teaching the child how to communicate. The current model proposes that the child is learning to communicate in every interaction, thus, SOs must learn to alter their spontaneous interactions to provide contingent models that match the child in ways he can assimilate. With this principle, the SO becomes aware of the regular functional effect her behavior has on the child's language and communication. She learns to look to herself first, rather than to other professionals, for answers to the question, "How can my child communicate better?"

2. The <u>systems principle</u> postulates that effective language teaching must involve not one theory, or one client, or one behavioral target at a time but several of each. That is, if language develops within a communicative system, its teaching must involve, as clients, all those persons currently in stable communicative relationships with the child and, as simultaneous targets, all those physical (mode), cognitive (form and content) and social (use and conversation) skills that comprise a next communicative level. When applied naturally, this principle insures that all significant persons know the rules of the teaching game. It also insures that teaching is not limited to single components as seen in the frequent "what's that?" teaching habit of parents and teachers, but that it also includes child, SO and conversation targets simultaneously.

3. The <u>child's world</u> principle stipulates that the SO's language teaching best begins in joint action with the child (Bruner, note 2; Snow 1978). Until the SO is actively <u>in</u> the child's action world, she will not be in a position to know the child's communicative intentions and language meanings. Often, SOs overshoot or underestimate the child's communicative competence when they fail to operate within the child's sensorimotor

domain (Moore and Meltzoff, 1978). With the Piagetian understanding that the child's actions represent his cognitive and communicative world, the model trains parents and teachers to use imitation, joint action and child feedback to first improve the perceptual match necessary for any mutual understanding and modeling. While the dictum, "be in the child's world", may appear to be a teaching principle too obvious to state, the consistent clinical observation of cognitive, perceptual, and communicative mismatches between delayed children and their caregivers makes it necessary to include this principle in the training of both parents and professionals. A major corollary principle is then to begin any assessment or training with the communicative modes, contents and intentions that are within the child's current competencies.

4.   Be conversational is a principle that underlies all assessment and training strategies within the current model. Based on the understanding that conversation begins in early infancy and requires no specific behaviors other than joint action or reciprocal attention to motor behaviors (Freedle and Lewis, 1977), this principle urges SOs to establish a conversational relationship with the child. In such a relationship SOs expect the child to communicate; they interpret his behaviors as communicative and respond accordingly. Specific strategies such as chaining the child's behaviors into mini-conversations and waiting for the child to communicate teach the child one of the critical first rules of communication development: to "give in order to get." Many handicapped children behave as though they do not know that if they give more of themselves socially, they will get more socially. Observations of the contingencies operating between the child and his SOs rarely provide evidence of give and take interactions in which both partners give and take with any reasonable balance. Moreover, upon interview, SOs show little understanding that conversations are necessary or even possible for language-delayed children. These SOs often do not follow the child contingently; they mismatch his mode, content and use; they communicate "rhetorically" and they perform with the child in ways that are likely to have little more than a superstitious or extinguishing effect on the child's emerging communication.

5.   The principle of <u>minimally discrepant modeling</u> integrates several learning principles. Modeling is a well established learning and teaching principle (Bandura, 1972) that states that an individual learns largely from the performances he observes naturally under no intentional teaching designs. The term <u>minimal discrepancy</u> (Hunt, 1961) refers to the theory that a child learns best if given models that are slightly more complex (minimally discrepant) than his stable performance on the skill in question. The principle suggests that a child will attend and learn best if the SO models communication that is not so advanced that the child will miss it perceptually, nor so close to the child's performance that he will be bored and not stimulated. Research on mother's speech to language-learning children (Broen, 1972) shows that the mothers studied usually spoke, paused, and restated in ways which accord well with the "minimal discrepancy" principle. Initial studies of parents of handicapped children do not support these findings but illustrate that they speak to their minimally verbal children with frequent long utterances and little waiting for a response (Rondal, 1978).

6.   The <u>new forms - old content</u> principle is extrapolated from cognitive learning theory and from work on cognitive prerequisites to language (Slobin, 1973). The principle states that new forms of behaviors (e.g. two word sentences, or action words) are first expressed in terms of old stable content (e.g. words or motor behaviors already in the child's repertoire). Applied to the task of language and communication training, this principle can be used to program targets across components in the system, for example, when the goal is teaching "action" words verbally. The "action" value specifies the content of the target, but what is the mode (one, two words, etc.), the use (e.g. answer, question), and the conversation value (e.g. imitation, response, turn length) that will be taught inadvertently or intentionally? The "new from old" principle would specify that if action words are the target, then they are best learned within the contexts of current modes, uses, and conversation structures. For example, a child will likely learn to use new action words e.g. run, eat, in old modes (e.g. single words) and esta-

blished uses (e.g. demand). The principle would argue not to model or expect two or more new components at once. In traditional practice, parents and professionals often test a child's language by asking (use) for a word (mode) about a referent (content) when the child has failed to master the answering skill (use), the word form (mode) or the semantics of the referent (content). The child's problems with language may well be due to the failure of the SOs to limit the number of new components of communication they expect at one time. Admittedly, this principle can best be used by professionals as they program sequences of targets for the child and SO. Through the model, SOs learn to identify the child's communicative mode, content, use and conversational skills and to alter one component at a time.

7. <u>Second Language Training</u> - The difficulty in teaching people to differentially attend to a child's nonlinguistic and linguistic communications is a problem that confounds the task of naturally teaching the child that there will be a greater payoff if he communicates in more conventional ways. Our consistent clinical observation is that SOs are seldom aware that they regularly accept immature idiosyncratic communications, thus giving the child neither reason to send his messages more conventionally nor clear signals as to how to send them. A strategy for such differential training is called <u>second-language training</u>. We instruct parents and teachers to treat the child's idiosyncratic communications as one language, and conventional communications as a second language. Then, the task is to respond to immature communication (e.g. pointing to refrigerator) by putting that message into a word or more conventional production that would be appropriate for the context. Thus, if a child points to a refrigerator, his mother might say "open," "food," "help" or any of a range of socially appropriate communications. Second language training can be translated into the natural operating rule, "put a word on the child's message." This principle also applies to earlier levels, where putting a gesture on a differential eye gaze, gives the infant-level child a more conventional expression for his message. The value we find in second-language training is twofold: first, SOs learn

to see language as developing from nonlinguistic and
idiosyncratic movements; and second, by second-language
training, the SO is capitalizing on the child's attentive moment to code for him a more conventional way of
communicating within that context.3

8.   Upping the Ante incorporates many of the principles as
     previously mentioned. Coined by Bruner (note 1) upping
     the ante involves requiring progressively higher com-
     municative levels from the child.   To quote Bruner:
         The   mother's   (often   quite   unconscious)
         approach is exquisitely tuned.   When the
         child responds to her 'Look!' by looking, she
         follows immediately with a query. When the
         child responds to the query with a gesture or
         a smile, she supplies a label. But as soon
         as the child shows the ability to vocalize in
         a way that might indicate a label, she raises
         the ante. She withholds the label and re-
         peats the query until the child vocalizes,
         then she gives the label.

9.   A final principle that, in its ideal expression, re-
     quires performance according to all of the above prin-
     ciples is the Gradual Balance of Power Shift.   Bron-
     fenbrenner (1979), in his treatise on an ecological
     theory of human development, asserts that the SO devel-
     ops along with the child in primary dyads. It is this
     dyadic development rather than child development that
     is central, and thus, one primary process for healthy
     development is the gradual shift in the balance of
     power from parent to child. Such a progressive balance
     requires that the parent be aware of what, how, and why
     the child is communicating so that she can yield to the
     child when he is likely to have new developmental
     successes. The model structures this balance of power
     through teaching SOs the contingencies that operate
     between them and their child.   Simply stated, they
     learn to determine if one person is running the com-
     municative show, then to use strategies to establish
     more of a shared turntaking relationship. Often, the
     parent needs first to re-establish her share of the
     power balance if she has come to be her child's non-
     contingent follower and has offered no model with sure
     contingencies to it. In most cases, it is assumed that

an interactive balance of power once existed during the
child's infancy. A series of situational and interactive strategies, such as play routines, communicative
match and waiting with anticipation, are used to teach
this progressive balance between SO and child that is a
foundation of conversation.

Strategies For Learning Communicative Expectancy

Three independent research programs investigating
mother-infant interaction (Brazelton, Koslowski, and Main,
1974; Freedle and Lewis, 1977; Lewis and Lee-Painter, 1974;
Lewis and Rosenblum, 1974; Stern, 1974, 1977; Stern, et al.
1975; and Stern and Gibbon, 1977) elaborately describe the
process of engagement and disengagement between mothers and
infants. Brazelton et al. (1974) report several ways in
which mothers come to have an expectancy for the child to
interact with them. Through fine tuning of the rhythm,
intensity, amplitude, direction and quality of her infant-
directed behavior, the mother attempts to elicit a signal
from the infant confirming that he is in touch with her.
The three research groups found patterns of prelinguistic
conversations in which the mother and child behaviors set up
predictable expectancies for the other to interact.

Interactions between handicapped children and their SOs
in our experimental program often reveal adults behaving as
though they do not expect the child to communicate or participate in the interaction. See Table 3 for script examples.
Frequently, parents and teachers are rhetorical, providing
neither the time nor the cues a child would need to respond.
These same SOs may regularly talk for the child, providing a
totally SO dominated conversation.

Early in each program, after SOs learn to observe key
communicative behaviors, they learn to interact as though
they expect the child to initiate, respond, and share turns
in conversations. They learn the strategies of waiting and
signaling for the child to communicate. They also reduce
their rhetorical communications and demonstrate through body
language and differential contingencies that they generally
expect the child to communicate. We have observed noncontingent rhetorical habits to extend even to physical prompts
of a child; SOs often interact with the child ambiguously as
though they were adding to every interaction a tag such as

"if you want to" or "if it's okay." Such weak pragmatic relations must be strengthened so that the child has clear unambiguous cues for communication.

Table 3

ILLUSTRATIONS OF EXPECTANCY VARIABLES

Script A
Minimal Expectancy

1. C REACHES FOR CEREAL
2. M "what do you want?" "cereal?"
3. C EATS CEREAL
4. M "good?" "sure, you like it"
   "tell me when you want more."
5. C CONTINUES EATING
6. M "ready for more?"
   "looks like it"
7. M takes bowl, fills it,
   returns to child
8. C EATS AGAIN
9. M "you are hungry"

Script B
High Expectancy

1. C REACHES FOR CEREAL
2. M gives quizzical look;
   holds box firmly
3. C "SI SI"
4. M "cereal?"
5. C "SI UL"
6. M "cereal!" "here"
   (pours in bowl)
7. M waits
8. C "muk"
9. M "milk--watch it fall on cereal"
10. M "now what?"
11. C "suga"
12. M "sugar in milk, now eat."

In Script A above, the mother's communication is generally rhetorical as she answers her own questions (2, 6) allows no time for a response (2, 4, 6, 7) and uses no signals for the child to communicate (2, 4, 6, 7). In Script B, the mother sets the stage for a more balanced conversation than that in A by waiting (2, 7) and signalling with (2, 5, 10) and without words (2), thus generally performing conversationally with the child, waiting for him to take his turn (2, 7) and chaining (4, 10) when necessary.

Interviews reveal that SOs' negative expectancies for the child to communicate may be related to their definition of communication in speech and language terms. Once SOs learn that their child will develop language on a continuum from nonlinguistic to linguistic communication, they come to expect more child-appropriate performances. They learn to actively show recognition that vocal and nonlinguistic behaviors are communicative. Subsequently, SOs learn to attend differentially in favor of new modes, contents and uses by following immature or null responses (failures to respond) with silence or reduced attention. In their interactions with the child, SOs learn to develop the self-fulfilling prophecy which sets a context in which all persons ideally wait, signal and generally expect the child to communicate. It is the reverse of the self-fulfilling prophecy described by Bateson (1964) when describing pathological communication. The current prophecy or response set allows for the child to participate in spontaneous conversations.

Language Teaching Strategies

A series of strategies have evolved to provide a pool of natural teaching strategies directed particularly to the task of improving the child's language components of mode, content, and use. Since any communication involves a mode(s), content and use, natural teaching strategies will have overlapping effects. But as we found in developing the curriculum, certain strategies were consistently effective in the individual task of training one of the components. The strategies include direct behavioral approaches, indirect context management and interactional approaches.

Mode

In terms of his communicative mode, the primary goal for a child is to bridge from idiosyncratic to conventional performance. Generally, SOs learn that, since any behaviors can communicate, their first task is to treat any new behaviors as communications until they are stable; afterwards they are to differentially attend to newer more conventional productions. Second-language training becomes habitual as adults use it to give the child more conventional models for his current communications. Imitation provides the child a model to which he can attend and teaches him that his communicative attempts will receive some response. Then, expansion models ways the child can change his performance toward conventionality. Imitation is used spontaneously to insure that the child has communicative feedback as to how his production was received. Frequently, we observe SOs make long interrogations as to their child's intentions when a simple imitation often yields more information and continuity to the interaction. In the model, imitation and expansions are used with several other strategies and never as a primary goal.

Modeling is regarded as a more effective and generalizable strategy for teaching language development than is imitation. The primary strategy used in modeling is "progressive match" by which the SO communicates slightly above the child's level following the minimally discrepant principle. In our experimental programs, parents and teachers learn to reduce their number of utterances and their mean length of utterances to the child's level. They give the child time to respond, then communicate with a close match to the child's mode, content and use. Frequently, we see totally linguistic SOs communicating without animation with a child who is primarily nonlinguistic. If maintained conversation is the ultimate goal and the process for language training, then SOs must be perceptually within the child's world so that he will stay with them for more natural language learning. Related to the issue of perceptually matching the child, SOs learn to change their mode of communication if their current mode yields no response. SOs are discouraged from repeating a question or command over and over; they are encouraged to change the mode to a more animated one or one closer to the child's performance.

Content

The issue of what cognitive or semantic content to train has been discussed earlier. The two directives that guide what to train are: 1) begin with meanings the child already communicates in an existing mode and then 2) to extend training to meanings that will be useful to the child in the task of making conversations out of social contacts. Thus, SOs learn first to experience the child's world as he physically does and to reference the child's current experiences and then learn to catalog the child's current communicative vocabulary (e.g. the meanings expressed with body language). Once they can identify the meanings (in words) the child communicates, they can begin second language training by putting words or more conventional communications onto the child's current communications. SOs are trained to respond to the child communicatively rather than to think and try to discover what the child really means. In programs designed primarily for communicative growth, "Put a word on his actions and communications" is a generally useful principle.

Use

The problem of how to teach pragmatics is receiving considerable attention (Hart and Risley, 1979; Hart and Rogers-Warren, 1978; Hubbell, 1981). A primary thesis of the present model is that a conversational milieu is needed with interactions designed for a variety of social contact purposes. In our programming, we have found it less fruitful to train particular speech acts than to establish and maintain conversations within a wide range of pragmatic interactions. Thus, SOs learn to contact the child for more reasons than before (e.g. to go beyond help and nurture contacts to ones that get information, give information, seek help, play and so forth).

We have found that a necessary and basic step in pragmatic training is to train SOs to treat the child's behavior as communicative providing communicative effects to child behaviors that, regardless of intention, may be shaped to more conventional or intentional communications. This merge of perlocutionary and behavioral principles predicts that those random child behaviors that consistently have communicative effects will come to be used intentionally to obtain similar effects.

Most parents and professionals also need to monitor and reduce rhetorical communication. Operationally defined in this model, a rhetorical communication is a message sent that neither cues nor allows for a response. For example, the mother who says without pausing: "Ready for school? Here's your hat, got your lunch? It's over there, see you later" is taking full responsibility for the conversation. If this rhetorical pattern is repeated habitually, the mother is teaching the child that his world will work just as well if he doesn't communicate. Consequently, the model recommends specific strategies that include the following: "communicate once, then wait with anticipation", avoid dead-end comments and a barrage of questions; practice nondemand intentions such as declarations and replies; and, perhaps most importantly, be interesting to the child. Become a generalized reinforcer whose very presence will cue social contact.

As seen in Table 4, scripts A and B contrast two approaches to communicating with a child. Script B is judged as incorporating several natural language teaching strategies while Script A violates several training principles.

In Script A, the mother misses two (1, 9) opportunities to treat the child's behavior as communicative. The mother in Script B capitalizes on similar opportunities (1, 7) and interprets his behavior as sending a message. In Script A, the mother fails to put words on the child's nonlinguistic communications (3, 7, 9) (second language training), and thus fails to give the child more conventional ways to communicate in those contexts. On the other hand, the mother in Script B, second language trains the child (4, 8) leading him into progressively more advanced communications even within the script. Mother A never imitates or expands the child's performance but stays in her own world. Where as, Mother B follows the child's communicative lead by coding his meanings (second language training) and imitating and expanding his utterances (6, 12). Finally, the two scripts differ strikingly in the way the two dyads match each other communicatively. Mother A communicates totally linguistically with an MLU of 5 words to a child who is primarily nonlinguistic. Her models both perceptually and cognitively overshoot the child's communicative and activity level. Mother B, however, appears finely tuned to the

child's linguistic level; her MLU of 2.7 compares favorably
with his of 1.0 especially because she also matches his
nonlinguistic communications (4, 9).

Table 4
LANGUAGE TEACHING STRATEGIES

SCRIPT A

1.	C	FINISHES CEREAL, PUTS SPOON ON TABLE
2.	M	"I'm not finished yet, sit there"
3.	C	SHAKES HEAD HORIZONTALLY
4.	M	"Oh yes you will"
5.	C	"NO"
6.	M	"Come on now, stay with me." I don't want you in there alone."
7.	C	STARTS LEAVING ROOM
8.	M	"Okay, just remember that when you want something."
9.	C	TURNS AROUND AND LOOKS AT M
10.	M	Makes no response

SCRIPT B

1.	C	FINISHES CEREAL, PUTS SPOON ON TABLE
2.	M	"More cereal?"
3.	C	SHAKES HEAD HORIZONTALLY
4.	M	Shakes head, "No more!"
5.	C	"NO MORE"
6.	M	"no more cereal"
7.	C	TURNS TO LEAVE TABLE
8.	M	"Go play?"
9.	C	"UH HUH" SHAKES HEAD
10.	M	"uh huh? Go play"
11.	C	"GO PA"
12.	M	"Go play, have fun"

Conversation Teaching Strategies

The model makes available to the SO a pool of strategies for use in training the child to operate successfully in conversations both with and without words. Before conversations begin the first strategy is for the SO to engage regularly in joint activities that offer give and take routines which can serve as generalization models for conversations in new settings. Once mutual attention and joint activity are established and maintained, SOs learn to increase the social contact purposes thereby providing more opportunities to keep the child interacting. SOs occasionally need to reduce certain contact purposes (e.g. to help, to give information) that may naturally lead to brief encounters and may limit conversation.

Then, SOs learn to take turns with the child often in three modes: nonlinguistically (e.g. physical play), vocally (e.g. sound games and imitation) and linguistically (with words). Turntaking is a deceptively simple skill. Maintaining and extending turntaking without dominating the exchange of communication or action is a difficult task for SOs who have been told to "talk to your child." A more effective dictum may be "take turns with your child." Turntaking, however, is not enough; conversation requires other skills as well. The SOs we observe questioning a child in a repetitive "what's that" turntaking routine are limiting the child's opportunity to take the active role that he must take if he is to incorporate the skills into his spontaneous repertoire. One particular strategy which can be used to engage the child and maintain conversations is the chain. Operationally, a chain is a response to one person that is also a cue for him to interact again. Recently, a nonambulatory child crawled to his father's feet and reached his arms up. Rather than lifting the child at once, the father said "what?" which chained the child into another communication, "up." Body language, intonations and any behaviors that serve to link the two into a continuous series of turns can serve as chains.

Once begun, conversations require certain strategies for their maintenance. SOs learn to apply these structural strategies within current topics or modes. The first strategy is to signal or mark turns for the child. For many handicapped children, the pause is insufficient as a cue to

take a turn. Waiting with clear visible anticipation is a
strategy that has been effective with our children usually
once the child has already learned turntaking routines.
Then, waiting becomes an essential strategy for both cueing
a turn and shifting the balance of power to the child for
his active participation. A third strategy is to respond
once, and then wait for the child to respond. Like the
waiting strategy, this strategy is necessary for SOs to
learn, in order to balance turns, so that a reciprocal
conversation can emerge.

Basic to natural conversation teaching are joint activities in which a child learns to take turns and in which he
learns he can take the lead at times. In script A (see
Table 5) the activity starts out as a directed almost didactic situation, not a joint activity with shared turns. The
mother fails to follow the child's interest in removing the
clothes. While the script may look like turntaking, the SO
and child are not sharing the activity. The mother is
generally rhetorical (1, 5, 10, 12) and fails to treat the
child's behaviors as conversational (6, 11) but responds in
ways that do not chain but rather depress the child's participation. Not only are the SO's communications not maintaining conversational chains, their linguistic complexity
prevents the child from understanding given his apparent one
or two word level.

On the other hand in script A, the mother establishes
the task as a joint shared activity from the beginning. The
mother treats the child's behaviors as communicative (3, 6,
11) and chains his behaviors into longer interactions (4, 6,
9, 12, 14). She also clearly signals when a turn is to be
taken (3, 9, 16). She generally shows she is conversational
by not being rhetorical, by chaining, by signalling for
turns, and by returning to the balanced turntaking cadence
when the child is distracted from the unspoken turntaking
rules. In fact, the mother appears to take a responsive
cooperative role with the child, a role that should teach
the child to keep responding and initiating in longer and
more complex conversations.

Summary

In the discussion, I have demonstrated how a new model
for early language intervention has evolved from several

TABLE 5
CONVERSATION TEACHING STRATEGIES

Script A
(emptying dryer)

1.	SO:	"let's empty the dryer!"
2.	SO:	stay here
3.	SO:	(removes clothing) "put this on the table"
4.	C:	(takes it to table)
5.	SO:	"now you want to take this one don't you?" (rhet.)
6.	C:	(looks at SO bewildered)
7.	SO:	"here, do it." (hands more clothes to him)
8.	C:	(puts it on the table)
9.	C:	(returns to dryer; puts hands in)
10.	SO:	"no, I'll give them to you
11.	C:	"me do"
12.	SO:	"you don't want to get in there"
13.	C:	(goes away to play alone)

Script B
(emptying dryer)

1.	SO:	"let's empty the dryer!"
2.	C:	(puts hand in dryer) "me do"
3.	SO:	"your turn"
4.	SO:	"What do you have?"
5.	C:	"daddy"
6.	SO:	"daddy's jammies? (points to table)
7.	C:	"jammie" - (puts clothes on table)
8.	C:	(returns to table)
9.	SO:	(intercepts him) who now?
10.	C:	(points to SO) "mamma"
11.	SO:	"mamma's turn" (takes clothes out)
12.	SO:	"what's this?" (holds clothes to child and waits)
13.	C:	"sissy"
14.	SO:	"sissy what?"
15.	C:	"sissy blanky" (puts it on table)
16.	SO:	"blanket like yours - my turn"

theoretical and empirical sources as they converged with our own findings from parent and classroom-based programs.

Two overriding premises of the approach were defined and operationalized in several ways. These premises are: that language emerges from natural conversations between the child and his significant others; and that intervention must involve both the child and his significant others in progressively matched and contingent conversations.

This model paper presents a system of child, conversation and significant other person variables as directions in response to the question; what to assess and train in children yet to develop a conventional communication system? In the system, the set of conversation targets is the central unifier of child and significant other targets. This conversational focus speaks to the now widely accepted and logical view that language acquisition requires an active conversational milieu (Bruner, 1978; Lewis, 1977; McLean and Snyder-McLean, 1978; Moerk, 1977; Snow, 1978; for example) in which the child learns to be conversational through chained turntaking and establishment of frequent progressively contingent conversations. A conversational environment differs from many therapeutic, educational and home environments in that, in the former, the adults become conversational partners in the child's world rather than teachers or caretakers who determine the goals and dominate the interactions in the latter.

As we further develop the model, we hope to uncover some common trends that appear to be irreducible and generalizable components across developmental classes of children and adults. At this point in the model's development, our initial findings suggest that a few components are critical to teaching language to a wide range of children. First, the idiosyncratic/conventional distinction appears consistent throughout families. That is, children have one communication system that works with their significant others (idiosyncratic) and another, much narrower one that strangers accept and understand (conventional). In all our applications of the model, we have trained parents and teachers to attend differentially to communications strangers would accept over the idiosyncratic ones that so limit his social and educational development. Thus, learning to attend to the child's various communication modes differentially is one hallmark of a communication vs. a language model.

Second, a series of strategies involved in "being contingently conversational" appear essential if the child's significant others are to become natural language teachers who are fine-tuned to the emerging modes, contents and uses of their child's communication (Bruner, 1978). Our almost ubiquitous finding is that parents, and often teachers, of a severely language delayed child regularly communicate rhetorically and take his communicative turn; that is, they expect him not to communicate in a certain way, then when the child fulfills their prophecy, the adults run the show and provide him inadequately matched signals and insufficient time to take his part in the turntaking exchanges necessary for language to emerge. Thus, turntaking becomes a critical skill and tool for natural language teaching.

A third consistent finding is that nearly all delayed children offer nonlinguistic communicative acts that are infrequently responded to in ways to shape them to more conventional productions. Parents and professionals need to come to an active awareness that speech and language will come from the child's nonlinguistic communicative acts. The finding that any behavior can become effective communication (Bates, 1976; Bruner, 1978; etc.) takes the vocal-linguistic pressure off the child whose physiology or history argues against current training. Logic would argue that the delayed child needs first to develop frequent and rich communications of any form, before going to a new structural level (e.g., vocal or linguistic). New forms (e.g., vocal or linguistic) will need to develop from old skills (e.g. nonlinguistic) that are soundly established and generalized broadly (Slobin, 1973). The rampant training on sounds and words seriously concerns me if it is done with children who do not yet have a spontaneous communication system within earlier physical modes. I fear that such training may have punitive, failure effects that may serve to erode what good communications he has and confuse him into functional social mutism.

What's next? Ongoing experimental work in classrooms and parent programs is attempting to determine clusters of targets for the child, the significant other and conversations that relate to both quantitative and qualitative

changes in children. This work should help to organize the
taxonomy into increasingly functionally related categories.
A basic question that is being asked is: when uninvolved
but experienced judges rate a video sample as high in con-
versationality, conventionality, communicative expectancy or
other global goals, what is occurring in the child, significant other and conversation events?

Because the model presents an ecological solution to
the problem of assisted language development, the next step
must involve communicating the model to and studying it with
the child's primary ecological managers, parents and teachers. Consequently, the model is being revised into three
curricular approaches. First, a curriculum, similar to that
described herein, is being revised for professional use with
individual parents. Secondly, the same curriculum is being
adapted for use by consultants who model and monitor it
within infant and preschool classrooms for developmentally
delayed children of all common diagnoses. A third direction
has recently evolved out of our finding that parents and
teachers need to learn to observe the critical components of
the child themselves and conversations before they will be
sufficiently motivated and skilled to become stable change
agents. To this end, we are designing a continuing education course directed to teaching parents and teachers to
"see" discriminately the range of child components involved
in his current idiosyncratic and conventional communication
systems. This preparatory curriculum will introduce the
series of events necessary for conversations to develop as
well as the natural teaching strategies of which adults are
frequently unaware, both of their existence and their effects on the child.

The work is exciting and overwhelming. Implications
may abound for populations other than severely delayed
children. Some corollary work has begun with adult apha-
sics. We will stay with our autistic, retarded, aphasic,
Down's syndrome and cerebral palsied children for now, and
invite others to explore the model on their own with these
and other children and their natural environments.

NOTES

[1]Throughout this model paper, "child" will be used to
refer to any individual whose language and communica-

tion performance is at developmental levels between birth and generalized conversational use of sentences. Thus, the model applies to all individuals within this range regardless of age.

[2]The Nisonger Center is one of several university affiliated programs for mental retardation and developmental disabilities. The programs are funded by the Maternal and Children Health Service of the U.S. Office of Education. The present model was also funded by a research grant from the Office of Special Education.

[3]While I recognize that the term 'language' is conventionally reserved for a culturally based symbolic system, its clinical ease and utility with parents and teachers have encouraged me to retain it for mnemonic and training purposes.

Acknowledgment:

The work represented in this paper was funded in part by an Office of Special Education grant, No. 6007801845.

REFERENCE NOTES

1. Bruner,   J.   Acquiring the use of language.   Paper
    presented at the Berlyne Memorial Lecture at the Uni-
    versity of Toronto, March, 1978.

2. Bruner,   J.   The role of dialogue in language aquisi-
    tion.   Paper presented at Conference on the Child's
    Conception of Language, Max Planck Society in Linguis-
    tics, Nijumegan, May 1977.

REFERENCES

Ainsworth, M.D.S.   The development of infant-mother attach-
    ment. In B.M. Caldwell and H.N. Picutti (Eds.), Re-
    view of child development research. (Vol. 3). Chicago:
    University of Chicago, 1973.

Almerico, T. and MacDonald, J.   The maternal pragmatic envi-
    ronment of replies and declarations in non-delayed and
    delayed children.   Unpublished Master's Thesis in the
    Dept. of Communication, The Ohio State University,
    1979.

Austin, J.   How to do things with words.   London: Oxford
    University Press, 1962.

Bandura, A. Modeling theory: Some traditions, trends and
    disputes.   In R.D. Parke (Ed.), Recent trends in
    social learning theory.   New York: Academic Press,
    1972.

Bandura, A.   Social learning theory.   Englewood Cliffs,
    N.J.: Prentice Hall, 1977.

Bates E. Acquisition of pragmatic competence. Journal of
    Child Language, 1974, 1, 277-81.

Bates, E.   Language and context: The acquisition of prag-
    matics. New York: Academic Press, 1976.

Bateson, G., and Jackson, D. Some varieties of pathogenic organizations. In David McK. Rioch, (Ed.), Disorders of communication, (Vol. 42) Research Publications: Association for Research in Nervous and Mental Disease, 1964, 270-83.

Bateson, G., Jackson, D., Haley, J., Weakland, J. Toward a theory of schizophrenia. Behavioral Science, 1966, Vol. 1.

Bentanfly, L. von. An outline of general system theory. British Journal of the Philosophy of Science, 1950, 1; 134-65.

Bloom, L. and Lahey, M. Language development and language disorders, New York: Wiley, 1978.

Blurton-Jones, N.G. Ethological studies of child behavior, London: Cambridge University Press, 1972.

Braine, M. Children's first word combinations. Chicago: University of Chicago Press, 1976.

Brazelton, T., Kaslowski, B., and Main, M. The origins of reciprocity: The early mother-infant interaction. In Lewis and Rosenblum (Eds.), Effect of the infant on the caregiver. New York: Wiley, 1974.

Broen, P.A. The verbal environment of the language learning child. ASHA Monograph No. 17, 1972.

Bronfenbrenner, U. The ecology of human development. Cambridge: Harvard University Press, 1979.

Brown, R. A first language: The early stages. Cambridge: Harvard University Press, 1973.

Brown, R. An introduction to Snow C. and Ferguson C. Talking to children: Language input and acquisition. London: Cambridge University Press, 1978.

Bruner, J. From communication to language, a psychological perspective. Cognition, 1974-75, 3, 255-277.

Bruner, J. Human growth and development, Wolfson College Lectures, 1976. Bruner and Garton (Ed.), Oxford: Clarendon Press, 1978a.

Bruner, J. Learning the mother tongue, Human Nature, 1978b, 42-48.

Bruner, J., Roy, C., and Ratner, N. The beginnings of request. In K.E. Nelson (Ed.), Children's language (vol. 3). New York: Gardener Press, 1980.

Bruner, J. The ontogenesis of speech acts. Journal of Child Language, 1975, 2, 1-19.

Chomsky, N. Syntactic structures. Mouton, The Hague, 1967.

Clark, E. What's in a word? On the child's acquisition of semantics in his first language. In T.E. Moore (Ed.), Cognitive development and the acquisition of language. New York: Academic Press, 1973.

Coulthard, M. An introduction to discourse analysis. London: Longman Group Limited, 1977.

Dore, J. Holophrases, speech acts and language universals. Journal of Child Language, 2, 1975, 21-40.

Dunst, C. A cognitive-social approach for assessment of early nonverbal communicative behavior. Journal of Child Communicative Disorders, 1978, Vol. 2(2).

Ervin-Tripp, S., and Mitchell-Kernan, C. Child discourse. Academic Press, Inc., 1977.

Ervin-Tripp, S. Wait for me roller-skate. In C. Mitchell-Kernan and S. Ervin-Tripp (Eds.), Child Discourse. New York: Academic Press, 1978.

Ferguson, C.A. and Farwell, C. Words and sounds in early language acquisition, Language, 1975, 51: 419-439.

Freedle, R. and Lewis, M., Prelinguistic conversations. In M. Lewis and L.A. Rosenblum (Eds.), Interaction, conversation, and the development of language. New York: Plenum Press, 1977.

Haley, J. Family experiments: A new type of experimentation. Family Process, 1962, 1: 265-93.

Haley, J. Research on family patterns: An instrument measurement. Family Process, 1964, 3: 41-65.

Halliday, M.A.K. Learning how to mean. In E.H. Lenneberg and E. Lenneberg (Eds.), Foundations of language development A Multidisciplinary Approach (Vol. 1). New York: Academic Press, 1975.

Harris, S.L. Teaching language to nonverbal children with emphasis on problems of generalization. Psychology Bulletin, 1974, 82, 525-588.

Hart, B. and Rogers-Warren, A. A milieu approach to teaching language. In R. Schiefelbusch (Ed.), Language intervention strategies. Baltimore: University Park Press, 1978.

Hart, B. and Risley, T. In vivo language intervention: Unanticipated general effects, Journal of Applied Behavior Analysis, 1979, No. 3, 407-432.

Hortsmeier, D. and MacDonald, J.D., Environmental prelanguage battery. Columbus: Merrill, 1978 a.

Hortsmeier, D. and MacDonald J.D., Ready set, go talk to me, Columbus: Merrill Publishing Co., 1978 b.

Hunt, J. Intelligence and experience. New York: Ronald Press, 1961.

Hymes, D. Models of the interaction of language and social life. In J.J. Brumperz, and D. Hymes (Eds.), Directions in socio-linguistics. Holt, Reinhart, and Winston, 35-71, 1972 a.

Hymes, D. On communicative competence. In J.B. Pride and J. Holmes (Eds.), Sociolinguistics. Harmondsworth: Penguin, 35-71, 1972 b.

Jackson, D. Communication, family, and marriage. Science and Behavioral Books, Palo Alto, 1968.

Lewis, M. and Lee-Painter S.   An interactional approach to the mother-infnat dyad.   In M. Lewis and L.A. Rosenbloom   (Eds.),   Effects of infant on caregiver.   New York: John Wiley and Sons, 1974.

Lewis, M. and Rosenblum, L.   Effects of the infant on its caregiver.   New York: Wiley, 1974.

Lewis, M.   State as an infant-environment interaction: An analysis of mother infant behavior as a function of sex.   Merrill Palmer Quarterly, 1972, 18, 95-121.

Lombardino, L., Willem, S. and MacDonald J.   Critical considerations in total communication and an environmental intervention model for the developmentally delayed.   Exceptional Children, 1981, 47(6).

Lombardino, L.   Maternal speech acts to non-delayed and Down's syndrome children: A taxonomy and distribution.   Unpublished doctoral dissertation, The Ohio State University, Colombus, Ohio, 1978.

MacCorquodale, K.   On Chomsky's review of Skinner's verbal behavior.   Journal   of the Experiemental Analysis of Behavior, 1970, 13, 83-99.

MacDonald, J.D.   Environmental language intervention: Programs for establishing initial communication in handicapped children.   In F. Withrow and C. Nygren (Eds.), Language and the handicapped learner: Curricula, programs, and media.   Columbus: Merrill, 1976.

MacDonald, J. and Horstmeier, D.   Environmental language intervention program.   Columbus: Charles E. Merrill, 1978.

MacDonald, J.D. and Blott, J.   Environmental language intervention: A rationale for diagnostic and training strategy through rules, context, and generalization.   Journal of Speech and Hearing Disorders, 1974, 39, 244-56.

MacDonald, J.D., Blott, J., Gordon, K., and Spiegel.   Experimental parent-assisted treatment programs for preschool language delayed children.   Journal of Speech and Hearing Research, 1974, 39, 395-415.

MacNamara, J. Cognitive bases of language learning in infants. Psychology Rev., 1972, 79, 1-13.

Madden, J., Levinstein, P. and Levinstein, S. Longitudinal outcomes of mother child home programs. Child Development, 1976, 47, 1015-1025.

Mahoney, G. An ethological approach to delayed language acquisition. American Journal of Mental Deficiency, 1975, 80, 139-48.

Mayo, C. On the acquisition of nonverbal communication: A review. Merrill Palmer Quarterly, 1979, 24(4).

McLean, J. and Snyder-McLean, L. A transactional approach to early language training. Columbus: Charles Merrill, 1978.

Mechlenberg, D. A group parent-based language training program for mentally retarded children. Unpublished Masters Thesis. The Ohio State University, 1976.

Mishler, E. Studies in dialogue and discourse III: Utterance structure and utterance function in interrogative sequences. Journal of Psycholinguistic Research, 1978, 7(4).

Moerk, E. Pragmatic and semantic aspects of early language development. Baltimore: University Park Press, 1977.

Moerk, E. Principles of dyadic interaction in language learning. Merrill Palmer Quarterly, 1972, 229-275.

Moerk, E. Processes of language teaching and training in the interactions of mother-child dyads. Child Development, 1976 47, 1064-1078.

Moore, M. and Meltzoff, A. Object permanence, imitation, and language development in infancy. Toward a Neo-Piagetian perspective on communicative and cognitive development. In E. Minifie and L. Lloyd (Eds.), Communicative and cognitive abilities in children. Baltimore: University Park Press, 1978.

Oller, D.K., et al. Infant babbling and speech. Journal of
    Child Language, 1978, 3: 1-12.

Owens, R. Pragmatic functions in the speech of preschool-
    aged Down's and nondelayed children. Unpublished
    doctoral dissertation, The Ohio State University, 1979.

Piaget, J. The language and thought of the child. World
    Publishing Co., 1971.

Rondal, J.A. Maternal speech to normal and Down's syndrome
    children. In E. Myers (Ed.), Monograph of the Ameri-
    can Association on Mental Deficiency, 1978.

Sacks, H., Schegloff, E.A., and Jefferson, G. A simplistic
    system for the organization of turn-taking for conver-
    sation, Language, 1974, 50(4), 696-735.

Schegloff, E.A. Notes on a conversational practice: Formu-
    lating place. In D. Sudnow (Ed.), Studies in social
    interaction, Free Press, 75-119, 1972.

Schiefelbusch, R. Bases of language intervention. Balti-
    more: University Park Press, 1978.

Schlesinger, I. Production of utterances and language
    acquisition. In D. Slobin (Ed.), The ontogenesis of
    grammar. New York: Academic Press, 1971.

Searle, J.R. Speech acts: An essay in the philosophy of
    language. New York: Cambridge University Press, 1969.

Seibert, J., Hogan. A. Procedures for the early social-
    communication scales, a working paper. The Mailman
    Center, University of Miami, 1980.

Sinclair, J. McH. and Coulthard, R.M. Towards an analysis
    of discourse. London: O.U.P., 1975.

Skinner, B. Science and human behavior. New York: Mac-
    Millan, 1953.

Skinner, B. Verbal Behavior. New York: Appleton-Century-
    Crofts, 1957.

Slobin, D. Cognitive prerequisites for the development of grammar. In D.I. Slobin and C. Ferguson (Eds.), Studies of child language development. New York: Holt, Rinehart, and Winston, 1973.

Snow, C. Mother's speech to children learning language, Child Development, 1972, 43, 549-565.

Snow, C. and Ferguson, C. Talking to children. London: Cambridge University Press, 1978.

Stern, D. Mother and infant at play: The dyadic interaction involving facial, vocal, and gaze behaviors. In M. Lewis and L.A. Rosenblum (Eds.), The effect of the infant on its caregiver. New York: Wiley and Sons, 1974.

Stern, D. and Gibbon, J. Temporal expectancies of social behaviors in mother-infant play. In E. Thoman (Ed.), The origins of the infant's responsiveness. New York: L. Erhlbaum Press, 1977.

Stern, D. The first relationship: Mother and infant. Cambridge: Harvard University, 1977.

Stern, D., Jaffee, J., Beebe, B., and Bennett, S. Vocalizing in unison and in alternation: Two models of communication within the mother-infant dyad. Annals of the New York Academy of Sciences, 1975, 263, 89-100.

Streml, K. and Waryas, C. A behavioral-psycholinguistic approach to language training. American Speech and Hearing Association Monographs, 1974, 18, 96-130.

Van Ek, J. The threshold level for modern language learning in schools. Longman Group Ltd., The Netherlands, 1977.

Watzlawick, P., Beavin, J. and Jackson, D. Pragmatics of human communication. New York: W.W. Norton, 1967.

Weinberg, G. Introduction to general systems thinking. New York: Wiley-Interscience, 1975.

Wells, G. Learning to code experience through language. Journal of Child Language, 1974, 1, 243-69.

Widdowson, H.G. An applied linguistic approach to discourse analysis. Unpublished doctoral dissertation, University of Edinburgh, 1974.

Wilkins, D. Grammatical, situational, and notional syllabuses. Paper presented to the Third International Congress of Applied Linguistics, Copenhagen, 1972.

Wilkins, D. Notional syllabuses and the concept of a minimum adequate grammar. In S.P. Corder and E. Roulet (Eds.), Linguistic insights in applied linguistics, Brussels, Paris, 1974.

6

INDIVIDUALIZED TEAM PROGRAMMING WITH INFANTS AND YOUNG HANDICAPPED CHILDREN

Philippa H. Campbell
Children's Hospital Medical Center of Akron

Programming for young handicapped children, while sometimes provided in the public schools, is more often delivered through private agencies, demonstration centers, hospitals, and other noneducationally based but publicly funded service providers (Vincent, Salisbury, Walter, Brown, Gruenwald, and Powers, 1980). Public schools have not widely adopted programming for infants and/or young handicapped children for a variety of reasons, including: lack of administrative expertise; lack of state and federal mandates; insufficient numbers of trained staff in early childhood/special education; inadequately validated models of service delivery appropriate for educational settings; insufficient funding levels to support such programs; and concern regarding noncomparable services for nonhandicapped young children (Hayden, 1979). Issues regarding location of services to be provided for infants and young children, however, are secondary to the more central concerns regarding the efficacy and cost-effectiveness of the service delivery models in practice today (Denhoff, 1981).

The most commonly adapted administrative structures under which services for young handicapped children have been delivered vary somewhat dependent on both the age of the child and the targeted geographical service delivery area. Infants (under the age of two years) are most frequently served through one-to-one intervention either in the home or at a central location. Toddler programs generally follow a classroom structure but group six to eight children together for instruction. During the preschool years most children with special needs will receive intervention in larger sized groups of 12 to 15 children that are a closer approximation in size to the kindergarten classrooms into which some young handicapped children will graduate (Safford, 1978). Service delivery models for providing occupational, physical, and speech and language therapies have been less clearly defined and adopted. Therapeutic interventions are often provided for handicapped children separate from the educational program rather than through models which would interrelate education, and therapeutic services. Outpatient models of one-to-one intervention where the child comes to a hospital, rehabilitation center, or other type of community based agency to individually receive needed therapy services remains the most typically implemented model of service delivery for children living in both rural and urban geographical areas. Therapists rarely are involved in home-based service delivery and are employed by educationally-based programs on a national basis to a much lesser extent than with out-patient treatment facilities (APTA, note 1).

Traditionally, the practice of occupational, physical, and speech and language therapies has followed a medical model of service delivery which includes both a diagnostic and treatment function. Coordination of the various therapeutic disciplines has been achieved through adoption of the concept of a team approach to service delivery. Multidisciplinary, interdisciplinary, and transdisciplinary team organizations (Hart, 1977) have been most prominent. These terms have not been precisely defined and therefore, have been used interchangeably in literature describing programming for handicapped children (Lyon & Lyon, 1980). These team organizations have been developed and practiced (but not validated for effectiveness) primarily in medical settings or within the context of the diagnostic-prescriptive model but do not easily transfer to educationally-based service delivery models (D. Bricker, 1976; Bricker & Campbell, 1980; Peterson, 1980).

The more severely handicapped the child, the earlier in the child's life a reliable medical diagnosis can be made (Beck, 1977; Hayden, 1979). The need for greater numbers of support services increases systematically in relation to the number of biological impairments that may be present. For example, a child with cerebral palsy who also has visual and hearing impairments requires the services of a greater number of specialists than does the child who is only hard of hearing (Orlando, 1981).

Traditionally, the public schools have not been mandated to serve the most severely multihandicapped students and subsequently have not had experience with employing or coordinating the wide variety of professionals who have the expertise necessary to plan and implement programming for students with multiple biological problems (Sternat, Messina, Nietupski, Lyon, & Brown, 1977). Private agencies and medically-based settings in which the more severely handicapped school-age child traditionally has been served have been on the forefront in development of infant and preschool services yet these agencies have not had much greater success in defining efficient methods for coordinating the number of professionals required to develop effective intervention strategies for handicapped children (Conner, Williamson, & Sieppe, 1978; Keough, 1973).

Service Delivery for Young Handicapped Children

An organizational structure which represents a variety of professional disciplines must be sufficiently flexible to account for the variety of factors which have an impact on service delivery (Garland, Stone, Swanson, & Woodruff, 1981). Location, child behavior (at any given point in time), ecology of the family unit, funding levels and sources, and model effectiveness are essential factors influencing the overall design of the service delivery model. Composition of the assessment-intervention team, coordination of expertise of those team members, and methods of interaction with the handicapped child and his family will be governed, in part, by the overall design of the service delivery model in use. Such a wide variety of service delivery models for young handicapped children are in use today as to preclude the extension and/or development of any one team organizational structure. For example, the so-called transdisciplinary or educational synthesizer models (D. Bricker, 1976) may be appropriate within some types of service delivery models or with some populations of handicapped children (for instance, infants) but less effective under other conditions (Campbell & Bricker, 1980).

Location

A number of characteristics which must be taken into account in service delivery can be considered under the general heading of location. Primary among these is the population density of the geographical area targeted for service delivery. Children who reside in sparsely populated geographical areas may be more efficiently served through types of service delivery that are not effective models for chil-

dren living in urban or suburban areas. However, the age of
the child to be served may also influence decisions about
whether services will be home-based, center-based, or a
combination of both locations. Bronfenbrenner (1975) concluded that very young handicapped children were more effectively provided with services in the home when orientation
of those services was toward training the parent(s) to be
effective interventionists with their children rather than
making the infant the exclusive target of service delivery.

A more recent consideration in service delivery models
concerns location in combination with which community agency
should be the provider of service for young handicapped
children. Public schools have been suggested for many years
as being the most ideal overall location for early intervention programs (Caldwell, 1972). The recent passage of the
Education for All Handicapped Children's Act, while not
directly mandating services for children below school-age,
has served as an impetus to encourage a greater number of
states to pass legislation requiring public school services
for young handicapped children (Cohen, Semmes, & Guralnick,
1979). To date, five states (Iowa, Michigan, Nebraska,
South Dakota, and Wyoming) have mandated services for handicapped children from the age of three years (Bureau of
Education, note 2).

Child Behavior

The individual patterns of strengths and impairments
demonstrated by a handicapped child potentially are alter-
able both through intervention and as a function of neuro-
developmental processes. Changes are more rapid and more
probable in infancy and, therefore, intervention is likely
to have the greatest effects on behavior of very young
children (Garland, Stone, Swanson, & Woodruff, 1981).
Targeted areas for intervention should change as the child
becomes chronologically older and as his behavior changes as
a function of intervention methods and procedures. Changes
in the behavior of handicapped children intersect with the
service delivery model in that the structure of services
provided must be flexible enough to accommodate developmental changes being produced. For instance, sensorimotor
skill development is likely to be a primary area of intervention provided for young children. However, the structure
of services must be able to change when, for instance,

communication or socialization become key areas of curriculum needs. Similarly, when selected intervention methods have not proven effective in altering the behavior of a given child, the clinician must utilize creative problem-solving to generate and validate strategies that can have an impact on behavior that has been resistant to change (W. Bricker, 1976). Common team organizational structures often do not allow for this necessary degree of flexibility and thereby act to prevent (rather than facilitate) an effective match between the required degrees of expertise, problem-solving, and knowledge and the severity of problems demonstrated by the child (Peterson, 1980).

Seldom is the characteristic of child behavior considered when designing service delivery systems for young children. More often, characteristics such as the age of the children to be served and the categorical descriptions assigned to various handicapping conditions are used as the primary bases for program design. For instance, service delivery systems may be designed to serve handicapped infants only or to serve only multihandicapped infants. Speech and language problems may be the targeted area of intervention for a particular service delivery model and children of all ages may be served through that model. Unfortunately, assignment of categorical labels to the multiplicity of factors (biological and environmental) that can potentially affect the process of development does not necessarily improve service delivery (Hobbs, 1975). For instance, lack of speech and language development can originate from biological and environmental factors (and more importantly, the interplay between the two) requiring somewhat different approaches for each child showing deficiencies in communication. An effective service delivery model must be responsive to the individual needs of each young child rather than to the global needs of a clinical group

Ecology of the Family Unit

Literature describing early intervention program design and methodology has traditionally focused on services delivered to the handicapped child. More recently, the importance of the child's position within a family unit has been emphasized (Anastasiow, 1981; Garwood, 1981). New interpretations of parental adjustment to having and raising a handicapped child are being proposed (Hayden, 1979). Some

of these approaches center on the amount and degree of
stress placed on the family attempting to raise a handicapped child (Bell, 1981). The traditional concept of the
two-parent family where the male is the primary support and
the female remains at home to care for the children and the
house is no longer the primary family unit in this country.
However, many early intervention programs for handicapped
children are designed with the assumption that the mother
will be able to transport her infant or young child to a
center or will be at home to receive the visits made by a
teacher or other professional. Services most often requested by parents of handicapped children include baby-
sitting, respite care, and community day care (Bromwich,
1981; Tjossem, 1976). Yet, these services are seldom provided by early intervention programs (Swan, 1980).

Coordination of medical, educational, and parent education services with day care and respite programs into family
centers has been suggested by Anastasiow (1981) as a holistic model of service delivery for handicapped children and
their families. The family center is similar to structures
and roles that have been suggested for implementation by
public schools (Bronfenbrenner, 1975; Caldwell, 1970)
although the more conservative viewpoint holds that schools
cannot be financially or programmatically responsible for
the wide range of components needed for comprehensive programs (Vincent & Bromme, 1977). The state of the art in
coordination of services provided by different agencies is
primitive, at best, and seldom effectively meets the needs
of the family to be served. However, any service delivery
model for young handicapped children must recognize the need
to coordinate provided services with the services of other
agencies if the total needs of the child and family are to
be met comprehensively (Garland, Stone, Swanson, and
Woodruff, 1981). Assigning case managers and/or child-family
advocates to assist the family in arranging for needed
services and coordinating the input from various service
delivery models has been suggested by individuals and in
some instances, is mandated by funding agencies.

Funding Levels and Sources

Early intervention programs are frequently referred to
by administrators as "labor intensive" due to the high
number of well-trained personnel that are required to pro-

vide adequate educational experiences for young handicapped children and their families. Educational administrative personnel, in particular, may be unaccustomed to operating programs which are staffed with low staff-child ratios. Public school personnel whose basis for comparison may be the ratios maintained for regular education (one teacher for 25-30 students) are particularly alarmed by what appears to be quite expensive programming. Despite the high costs of effective programming, many sources exist for finding infant, toddler, and preschool programs, including a variety of federal and state fiscal programs in both health care and education.

Realistically, the amount of funding available to an agency providing services to young children is probably the most significant determiner of the service delivery model. Frequently, program offerings are based more on budgetary considerations than on the comprehensive needs of the population targeted for service (Campbell, note 3). The unfortunate fact is that "...the more expensive programs have produced the more impressive results. If the data are to be taken seriously in formulating a national policy, economic feasibility is inevitably an issue. It is paradoxical that as a rich country we make decisions about military spending in terms of national security needs, whereas decisions about education are made not in terms of needs but of costs" (Horowitz & Paden, 1973, page 392).

No national mandate for providing comprehensive services for young handicapped children exists. However, funding is potentially available through a diverse number of public and private sources, each of which has regulations and guidelines regarding expenditure of funds. Potential problems arise where children who qualify for intervention through one funding source may be eligible for services that are denied other children enrolled in the same program. Lack of coordination among public and private funding agencies at both the federal and state levels makes coordination at the local level at best difficult, and more often, impossible. Just as the service delivery model for a given program may be defined by the amount of funds secured, the services provided and their organizational structure may be regulated directly and indirectly by funding source guidelines rather than on the basis of comprehensive planning of empirical evidence. For instance, transdisciplinary team organization is difficult to institute if third party payers reimburse for individual units of therapy or have limits on the number of units of service that can be billed during a given time period. Similarly, transdiciplinary programming is often recommended' for classroom-based programming for handicapped children due to difficulties in obtaining manpower with necessary therapeutic expertise (Bricker, Sheehan, & Littman, 1981; Lyon & Lyon, 1980).

Model Effectiveness

A variety of models for delivering services for young handicapped children have been proposed and instituted, but few of the existing models have been validated for effectiveness of intervention procedures (D. Bricker, 1978; Denhoff, 1981; Peterson, 1980). Even fewer studies have been made of the cost effectiveness of delivering services to young handicapped children (Swan, 1980). The need for documentation of effectiveness of intervention both empirically and financially is immediate and critical. Yet, few community based programs are designed to document effectiveness and few include either the staff expertise or financial latitude to invest resources in methodologically sound program evaluation (Bricker, Sheehan, & Littman, 1981).

A number of articles have been published which question the validity of early intervention (Caputo, 1981; Denhoff, 1981) or question the value of intervention with specific populations of handicapped children. However,

> ....There are numerous methodological problems which make this question (cost effectiveness) difficult to answer. For example, the cost per child may vary by year because of increasing age, because of changes in the handicapping condition, or because educational or maturational effects warrant new educational programs. Another problem in determining cost effectiveness of early intervention programs is the lack of compatible record-keeping systems and cost data from program to program. Finally there is the problem of variable costs for both handicapped and nonhandicapped education across the country. (Garland, Stone, Swanson, & Woodruff, 1981, page 15).

Lack of data which substantiate the effectiveness of early intervention program models has not yet had a significant impact on the numbers of programs available or their funding levels. However, concerns regarding effectiveness in general, utilization of personnel, cost-effectiveness, and benefits of specific educational and therapeutic approaches and procedures are beginning to be addressed in professional journals. Individuals involved in delivery of services for young handicapped children must undertake responsibility for more than just serving children and families. They must accept the responsibility for demonstrating the effectiveness of their services.

Team Effectiveness Within Service Delivery Models

Virtually no research has been completed which documents either the effectiveness of one type of team organizational structure over another or recommends an organization of therapists and other support personnel in relation to a particular service delivery model being implemented. Most recommendations for various types of team organizational structures are made on the benefits to the participating professional staff rather than on the benefits to the recipients of the team approach being advocated (Albano, Cox, York & York, 1981; Connor, Williamson, & Sieppe, 1978; Peterson, 1980). Furthermore, few recommendations are made with consideration to other characteristics of the service delivery model such as population served, location, effectiveness, and funding (Connor, Williamson, & Sieppe, 1978; Peterson, 1980; York, & York, 1981). Part of the confusion in even subjectively judging the effectiveness of various team organization structures stems from the attachment of further labels describing location where the team member delivers services and primary role of team members. For instance, frequently, both the multidisciplinary and interdisciplinary models are described as being provided in isolated settings whereas integrated settings are specified as the location for the transdisciplinary approach. Also, the multidisciplinary and interdisciplinary models are assumed to include only direct intervention but indirect intervention (through another person) or consultative monitoring are illustrated as the key components of transdisciplinary programming (Lyon & Lyon, 1980; Sternat et al., 1977). A program that operates on the basis of information sharing and with the designation of a key team member as the

primary therapist or programmer, components of the so-called
transdisciplinary model (Hutchinson, 1978), can provide
direct intervention in isolated settings. Programs organized around interdisciplinary models may be involved in
providing parent training or other functions which place
team members in a consultative role.

A "one best" team intervention model, designed to meet
the needs of all types and ages of handicapped children and
their families, residing in any geographical location, with
a variety of educational and socioeconomic backgrounds, and
with differing degrees of stress on the family unit has not
yet been devised. More important is an awareness that such
a model, in actual practice, will emerge as a series of team
models which comply with the characteristics of the service
delivery approach as a whole. Once such models are designed
and implemented, testing must occur to validate the effectiveness of team programming in producing differential and
measurable effects on the behavior or development of the
recipient of those services.

> The better and more efficient the team, the better
> the services offered to the child. No matter what
> approach used or the type of team involved, the
> better the expertise and the greater the willing-
> ness of the team members to share information, the
> greater the benefits for the child (Hart, 1977, p.
> 396).

Positive change in attitudes of team members or more cooperative working relationships among the various disciplines
are positive products of an effective team. These cannot be
judged as fully meaningful unless that cooperative spirit
produces positive change in the behavior of the children who
are the focus of the team's planning.

Programming for Handicapped Young Children

An individualized approach to provide team programming
for young handicapped children and their families has been
implemented. This program is currently being tested and
validated within a service delivery system based on decisions made in relation to each of the characteristics of
service delivery models.

Location

The program serves children from birth to six years of age and is located within an elementary school which also houses a developmental day care and preschool program for children, 3 to 6 years of age. The elementary school is operated by Kent State University as a laboratory school for teacher training but also is classified as a public school. Students come to programs located at the school from a variety of school districts surrounding Kent, Ohio and represent the diverse professional and socioeconomic backgrounds of individuals who reside in northeastern Ohio. School districts provide transportation for the elementary aged students but the preschool and younger children are transported by their parents. Children do not have to reside within specified geographical boundaries to participate in the school's programs.

The Early Intervention Program focuses service delivery on handicapped children and their families, providing infant-toddler, toddler, and preschool classes using a reverse mainstreaming model (Turnbull & Blancher-Dixon, 1980) where non-handicapped age mates also participate in classroom-based instruction. Handicapped children attend the Child Development Center program which is organized around age-based classroom units for 3, 4, and 5 year olds. Degree of participation ranges from partial to full half-day attendance using a traditional model of mainstreaming where the majority of children in any classroom are non-handicapped (Guralnick, 1978). The development of the Early Intervention Program and its location at the University School was systematically undertaken to integrate handicapped and non-handicapped children, but also because its location is ideal in that the program draws from rural and urban schools thus facilitating future replication of the service delivery model.

Child Behavior

Three central themes guide the organization and operation of the Early Intervention Program: training of education and related services personnel in effective team-based programming; implementation of applied research projects designed to measure the effectiveness of specific intervention approaches with handicapped children; and demonstration

of an effective model of service delivery for young handicapped children and their families. The program is designed
not just to serve children and their families but to develop
and validate innovative practices for remediating and alle-
viating the effects of handicapping conditions on developmental processes. Change in the behavior of the children
served is the standard that governs all decision-making
processes and ties together the research, training, and
demonstration functions of the overall service delivery
model. The goal of team-based services is to create change
in the developmental processes of each child through pro-
moting skill acquisition in a variety of behavioral and
developmental domains. Skills must be definable, measurable, in order to objectively judge if acquisition has
occurred.

Ecology of the Family Unit

The Early Intervention Program philosophy suggests
family members will have a significant impact on the handicapped child's behavior. Some children participating in the
program are part of single parent family units while others
are from families in which both parents are employed. Also,
the majority of families contain other young children. The
diversity in family education, socio-economic background,
number of children in the family, and other factors demanded
the development of services for parents that would be flexible enough to encourage participation on a variety of levels
while structured enough to provide families with skills
necessary to both instruct their children and advocate for
rights to quality programming and services. Program services were initially designed by program staff but currently
are largely developed by the parents of the children. These
services include education, training, information, and
support-counseling activities which, hopefully, alleviate
the stress that is often added to the family unit by the
presence of a child with handicapping conditions. Parents
are key members of the team and have equal responsibility
for developing program goals. Communication with the parent
is enhanced by participation in all team planning and implementation of activities both in the school and at home.
Some parents are very involved in providing instruction for
their children at home, while others are not. Most often,
families who do not provide much systematic instruction at
home are those with two working parents and a number of

young children who require a great deal of care. The unique circumstances of each family are given every consideration when Early Intervention Program Staff develop individual program plans. An overriding focus of all plans is to alleviate stress within the family unit.

Funding Levels and Sources

Each of the program components of the University School have different funding bases. The Early Intervention Program is largely funded through a series of federal grants which focus on research, demonstration, and interdisciplinary personnel preparation. The Child Development Center is partly subsidized by the Department of Early Childhood, Kent State University, and hourly fees paid by the parents of children attending the program or by third party payers (such as welfare departments). The elementary school program receives partial subsidy from the College of Education, public education dollars (state allocation for public schools), and small tuition payments made by parents. None of the parents of children attending the Early Intervention Program are charged for services provided. However, parents have undertaken a variety of fund-raising activities which provide most supplies and materials required for program operation. In addition, parents have established a fund which offsets costs for handicapped children attending the Child Development Center.

None of the programs operating at the University School have excess funds nor does any program have the capability of raising funds through public levies. Early childhood education for handicapped children is not mandated in Ohio and, therefore, state funding to support these activities is minimal. Federal monies to demonstrate effectiveness of services, to support applied research efforts, and to train educational and therapeutic personnel have remained the primary base of support.

Model Effectiveness

Demonstrating and validating an effective model of team intervention with young handicapped children is, in the Early Intervention Program, not just an add-on to delivery of services, but an essential component of program design.

Therefore, the ways in which services are delivered, personnel are organized, and funds are utilized are all flexible.
The allocation of resources is adjusted as needed and in
relation to change in the behavior of the children being
served through the program. Program organization, structure, content, and methodology are all changed when data
indicate that the children are not changing as a function of
intervention being provided. The result has been a program
which emphasizes individualized team programming as a re-
placement of the more traditional interdisciplinary, transdisciplinary, and multidisciplinary models of team intervention.

The Individualized Team Model

The structure and composition of a team of individuals
whose goal is to produce change in the behavior of the child
served is quite different from standard team model goals
that focus on the process rather than the product of the
model. The transdisciplinary model focuses on methods of
role release (Lyon & Lyon, 1980), or of facilitating communication among team members (Peterson, 1980) or of assigning
responsibility of primary programmer to one team member
(Hart, 1977) who in educational environments is most often
the teacher (Albano, Cox, York, & York, 1981; D. Bricker,
1976). Efficient organization in relation to assessments
(Orlando, 1981) or accuracy of assessment results when
translated into programming goals (Bricker & Campbell, 1980;
Beck, 1977) are frequently cited in discussions of multidisciplinary and interdisciplinary teaming structures. Considerable effort has been directed toward role delineation of
team members in all three standard approaches.

The organization of the individualized team approach
differs from the interdisciplinary, multidisciplinary, and
transdisciplinary models in that flexibility is essential.
The number of disciplines of team members represented on the
team at any moment in time can differ with one exception,
that is, the parent is always a member of the team. The
rest of the team is made up of individuals with expertise
necessary to plan and implement programming required by the
child and family at any point in time. Team members provide
direct and, where appropriate, isolated intervention but
also function in consultative-teaching roles to other individuals on the team including the parent(s). The structure

and composition of the team remains constant as long as the product of the team's efforts, change in the child's behavior, is being achieved. Regrouping of team members (including adding/subtracting members of particular discipline backgrounds) occurs when the child's instructional and therapeutic priorities change sufficiently to require additional expertise not previously included on the team, the family situation changes, or the behavior of the child does not show sufficient change (indicating the need for more careful analysis of intervention strategies being implemented). Therefore, team organization may be structured so that various team members take on greater responsiblity for direct child programming during a time period where the family does not have sufficient resources to devote to training their handicapped child. These instances have included arrival of a new baby in a family with a severely multihandicapped two year old or high periods of stress such as illness, death, divorce, or other problems. Similarly, team members may focus on parent training sufficient to enable the family to be the primary instructors of their young handicapped child in order to teach skills (such as independent toileting) that are quite difficult to teach only during a classroom day.

A young infant with difficulties with movement may be adequately treated by a team consisting of the parent and a professional. When other biological impairments are present; treatment may also require such specialists as a vision training teacher, an audiologist, teacher of the hearing impaired, or a physician. Where the infant has specific difficulties, such as feeding problems, a speech clinician or occupational therapist's expertise may be required in order to establish programming and effective home feeding procedures designed to improve functioning in the oral-motor musculature. A nutritionist may be necessary to assist the family in meal planning with their infant. The "ideal team model", then, is not interdisciplinary, multidisciplinary, or transdisciplinary but individualized such that the expertise necessary to generate and deliver instructional and therapeutic strategies that teach the handicapped child to function at home, at school, and in the community is contained on the team at all points in time. Team membership becomes defined by the needs of the child and his family at any moment in time rather than by which professionals comprise a particular program.

Theoretical Bases

    One of the difficulties frequently encountered by team
models is that team members do not agree on and/or do not
adhere to similar theoretical bases from which programming
targets and strategies are derived (Albano, Cox, York, &
York, 1981). Furthermore, many disciplines are not based on
a uniform theory of development and/or originate from a
basis of the maturational model of development and/or originate from a basis of the maturational model of development
(Campbell, in press). Each member or potential member of an
individualized team must agree on an overall theoretical
basis from which programming targets and strategies will be
derived. This will insure a strong relationship between
assessment and programming providing a basis against which
the overall effectiveness of potential intervention strategies can be measured.

    Team members agree to program on the basis of a Pia-
getian approach to child development but use a framework of
applied behavior analysis for generation of specific instructional strategies (see Figure 1). The model was constructed in terms of movement (motor skills) since many of
the children attending the program have difficulties with
movement as a result of damage to the central nervous system. Piagetian labels for the developmental schemes were
changed to reflect this emphasis (primary circular reactions
became primary movements). This movement perspective also
mandated the inclusion of automatic movements within the
model. These movements are used to right the body in space
and maintain balance against changing gravitational conditions. The outcomes of a dysfunctional central nervous
system in terms of movement disorders were also added as
underlying components of movement to emphasize that problems
with postural tone, quality of movement patterns (form of
movement), and rate of movement were derived from central
nervous system damage but were components of any type of
movement to be expected from the child. Whereas this type
of theoretical intervention model is most useful with young
children with movement difficulties, the model applies to
children with other types of problems as well.

    The general theoretical model not only provides a stan-
dard and agreed-upon basis for child programming but also
organizes the expertise of various disciplines that may be

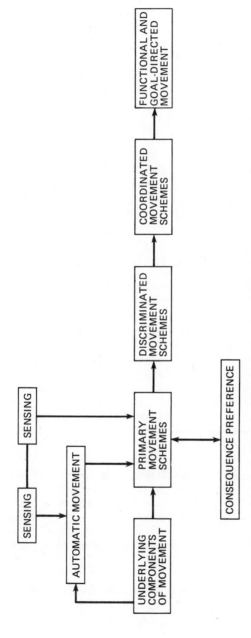

Figure I. Model of intervention for children with motor impairments

needed to both develop and deliver programming for young
handicapped children. For example, an individual with
training in movement skills, i.e., typically the physical or
occupational therapist is likely to have more knowledge
about underlying components of movement than he has in other
areas of development. However, movement therapists will
need assistance from other team members (including parents)
to identify the motivational conditions necessary to instate
primary forms of movement with handicapped children. Furthermore, information about visual processes and functioning
may be needed to generate appropriate and effective strategies to teach automatic movement patterns to a child with
severe visual impairment. The model can be expanded (see
Figure 2) to provide more detail in each of the major areas
and can be used as the basis for developing long-range goals
for specific children and in specific areas of programming
directed toward developing goal-directed (intentional)
movement.

Assessment-Programming: Test-Teach Intervention

The individualized team model includes both an assessment and intervention component. However, these two components are not implemented exclusive of each other as is
often the case with standard teaming models where each
discipline performs an initial evaluation separate from the
evaluations performed by other disciplines (Albano, Cox,
York, & York, 1981; Hart, 1977). Rather, the assessment and
intervention phases are combined as is necessary when programming decisions are made on the basis of objective child
performance data (Haring, Liberty, and White, 1980). The
emphasis of the assessment process is on the identification
of possible strategies that will be effective in generating
child change rather than on the numbers of problems/weak-
nesses that the child may have, the developmental or mental
age, or current degree of skill attainment in any developmental or behavioral domain.. Measures such as these, whether made for the purpose of instituting programming, as is
the case in the diagnostic-prescriptive models, are failure-
oriented (Keough, 1973) and do not provide a direct bridge
to intervention (Keough & Kopp, note 4).

Initial areas of programming emphasis are identified in
the individualized team model on the basis of the theoretical model underlying team intervention in combination with

Figure 2

DETAILED MODEL OF INTERVENTION FOR CHILDREN WITH MOTOR IMPAIRMENTS

SENSING:
- VESTIBULAR
- VISUAL

SENSING:
- VISION
- HEARING
- PROPRIOCEPTION
- TOUCH

AUTOMATIC MOVEMENT:

- BRING BODY PARTS
  INTO ALIGNMENT
- BRING AND MAINTAIN
  BODY ALIGNMENT IN
  RELATION TO GRAVITY

UNDERLYING COMPONENTS
OF MOVEMENT:

- POSTURAL TONE
- RATE OF MOVEMENT
- FORM (QUALITY) OF MOVEMENT

PRIMARY MOVEMENT SCHEMES

- SIMPLE MOBILITY
- UNCONTROLLED ARM MOVEMENTS
- HOLDING (GRASP)
- ORAL MOVEMENTS IN EATING
- ORAL MOVEMENTS IN VOCALIZATION

CONSEQUENCE PREFERENCE

FUNCTIONAL AND
GOAL-DIRECTED MOVEMENT:
- COMMUNICATION
- MOBILITY
- ARM AND HAND MOVEMENT
- MANIPULATION SCHEMES
    VOCATIONAL
    RECREATIONAL
    SELF-CARE
- SOCIAL INTERACTION

parent-identified areas of concern. Staff and parent-identified areas of emphasis are discussed in combination with
possible ways in which program resources can be organized
and delivered to produce skill acquisition. Severely handicapped children may require organization of resources that
provide a great deal of one-to-one systematic instruction
and therapy whereas the instructional needs of less handicapped children may be able to be met largely through classroom and small group instruction. Initial programming
decisions will be altered when child behavior changes or
does not change as a function of the organization of program
resources.

Members of the individualized programming team collect
child performance data regularly on all instruction or
therapy being provided and evaluate the data at least
weekly. The evaluation of the effects of specific intervention strategies through objective data allows each team
member to determine the extent to which programming being
provided for an individual child is effective. The emphasis
in programming is both on testing the effectiveness of
instructional strategies being implemented and teaching the
child new skills. Those strategies that do produce changed
child behavior are continued while those that do not result
in substantial and positive alteration are eliminated and/or
modified or replaced with alternate strategies. Consistency
in implementing instructional and therapeutic strategies
across people and contexts can be checked using the objective data. Parents can assist in data collection in the
classroom and can collect data on similar or different
instructional targets while working at home. Parents may
also become involved in collecting observational data representing the child's performance under less structured and
more natural conditions.

Initial assessment-programming targets are identified
by the parent and the team following the child/family initial visit. Typical targets involve instructional programming needs in goal-directed forms of behavior such as communication, mobility, upper extremity and manipulation
skills in play and self-care activities, and other functional and chronologically age-appropriate skills. Additional targeted areas may include normalization of postural
tone, training in performance of normalized patterns of
movement, and increase/decrease in the rate of movement

exhibited by children with disorders in movement derived
from central nervous system damage. These areas of movement
which underly the ability to perform within a normalized
environment may be targeted for direct and individual intervention (through physical and occupational therapy) and/or
may be incorporated into all activities undertaken with a
child by the team members. The overall objective of assessment-programming is to insure that the child acquires critical and functional skills in the shortest time possible.

Strong Inference Testing

Some children, particularly those with severe and/or
multiple impairments, may neither readily nor easily acquire
functional skills using standard practice intervention techniques derived from psychology, speech and language therapy,
motor therapies, or education. The structure and organization of the team must allow for sufficient time for each
individual team member to utilize problem-solving strategies
or hypothesis testing activities designed to identify more
effective ways of intervening with children whose behavior
does not become substantially altered under standard intervention conditions. Strong inference testing (Bricker,
1976) encourages the formulation of possible reasons (hypotheses) why a child may not be acquiring a targeted skill
and provides the basis for further test-teach programming as
a means of identifying factors which are influencing instructional and therapeutic success. Strong inference
testing should be implemented as soon as the data being
collected on child performance on any targeted skill area
indicate that the intervention procedures being utilized are
not effective in changing the behavior of the child in
predicted directions.

Strong inference testing is implemented by the team
members in two phases. The first phase involves a review of
the data collected on an individual instructional or therapeutic target that is being implemented with either an
individual or a group of children. The team determines and
formulates a list of possible reasons why the data are not
being substantially altered in a positive direction. Hypotheses may include child-specific reasons or may include
reasons relating to overall ineffectiveness of techniques or
methods being implemented. All team members who have expertise related to a particular instructional area or program

being subjected to <u>strong</u> <u>inference</u> <u>testing</u> must have input
into the formulation of the hypothesis list either at a
general team meeting (if time allows) or through simply
providing a list to one individual who has been designated
to coordinate the testing phase. The general team meeting
has some advantages in that input from some team members may
act as a catalyst for other members. However, the meeting,
itself, is not essential to the <u>strong</u> <u>inference</u> process.

   The second phase of testing includes direct implementation of training procedures that will provide additional
data in relation to the hypothesis being tested. For instance, with one student who was being trained to look at a
picture of his mother in the presence of a blank distractor
(using a two-choice discrimination paradigm) the team hypothesized that the student was correct in looking at his
mother's picture because the picture was colored (and being
paired with a non-color distractor). Therefore, in order to
rule out a hypothesis that the student was looking at color
(and not at a picture of his mother), the team paired the
picture of his mother with a same-sized colored picture of
an object. The data indicated that the student continued to
look at his mother's picture when requested to do so, indicating clearly that visual recognition was present (see
Figure 3).

FIGURE 3

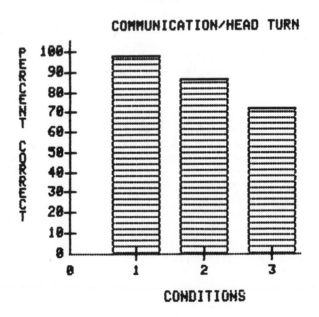

COMMUNICATION/HEAD TURN

Replication of Effective Strategies

The result of test-teach and strong inference testing procedures is team-generated and tested strategies which are documented as effective in training particular children to perform specified behavioral functions. Many children with severe and multiple handicaps can be instructed to perform particular targeted skills using the same or very similar procedures. Procedures that have been validated as effective with one child should be implemented to train similar behavioral functions with other children who require training in those areas. Too often, handicapped children are viewed by team members as unique and different from all other children. Therefore, new approaches or procedures are often tried with students on a hit-or-miss basis. This process can frequently not only frustrate staff and parents because of lack of success but also penalize the handicapped child by wasting valuable training time.

Replication of effective training and therapy strategies can occur with children as a group and/or on a child-by-child basis. For instance, when several students with similar characteristics have been identified with similar instructional needs in a particular area, the same procedures can be implemented with each student. Stimulus materials may be different for each student but the manner of presentation (the antecedent conditions), the reinforcement process (continual, intermittent, etc.) and the manner of collecting and recording data should be held constant. Team members then are able to judge effectiveness on both a child-by-child basis as well as on a group basis. In other situations, where procedures have been utilized in training only one student, if effective, these can be re-implemented with other children when their instructional needs indicate skill training in the same area. An outcome of the replication process is that the team, in essence, designs an effective curriculum for training children to perform functional skill acquisition and saves valuable time by not having constantly to redesign and rewrite individual training programs for each child.

Individualized Team Programming In Communication
Training With Very Young Severely Handicapped Children

Four children at the Early Identification Program were
identified with needs for communication training. Each of
these children were diagnosed as cerebral palsied and each
had received visual assessments which indicated questionable
visual acuity. Each student had a unique and limited number
of identified reinforcing objects, foods, or activities.
The particular characteristics of movement dysfunction
included severe hypertonia with no voluntary movement of the
extremities, fluctuating tone ranging from hypotonia to
hypertonia with limited and uncontrolled movement of the
upper extremities (two children), and severe hypotonia with
limited movement of the upper extremities against gravity.
The age of the students ranged from 2-10 years to 5-9 years
with a mean age of 4-3 years.

A team consisting of a visual specialist, physical
therapist, occupational therapist, speech/language clinician, and parents formulated a general training strategy
believed to be an effective method for initiating training
in nonverbal communication using a visual attention-to-
named-picture response (Figure 4). A two-choice discrimination paradigm using a picture stimulus paired with a blank
distractor card was used for training. Two baseline performance conditions were implemented to assess behavior with
standard-vocabulary; line drawings of face, cup, television,
boat, and shoe (initial baseline condition); and individual-
ized-vocabulary line drawings representing objects known to
be preferred by each student constituted the second baseline
condition. Training was implemented with each student using
the preferred-object line drawings.

The performance of these students as a group is represented in Figure 5. Data indicated that the students did
not visually attend to standard-vocabulary line drawings any
more frequently than they attended to familiar individual-
ized-vocabulary items. Performance under training conditions increased above baseline behavior. However, gains
were not substantial and did not occur across all students.
The individualized programming team implemented strong
inference testing with three of the children in order to
identify those conditions which would produce increased use
of eye pointing responses as an initial basis for nonverbal
communication. The fourth student was discontinued from

Figure 4

EYE POINT TRAINING PROCEDURE

Child's Name: _____
Date Initiated: _____

Required Response: An eye point is considered to occur if the child's eyes make visual contact (fixation) with the grid section in which the named stimulus is presented for 3 seconds; within 15 seconds of verbal antecedent.

Enter

Trainer presents designated object to child, trainer interacts with child and object (functional use of object) for 30 seconds

Trainer removes object and presents picture of object and blank card saying: "Lets play with the _____ again. Look at the picture".

Child is allowed 15 second latency to look at the picture. Does the child look at the designated picture? 3 seconds

no → Trainer cues child by pointing to picture or moving hand near picture saying "Here it is"

Does child look at the designated picture with movement cue?

no → Physically guide child to look at picture. When child looks at picture say "Good, that's the picture".

yes

Trainer brings object into view (low key) saying "Yes, here's the _____." 5 seconds

Trainer removes object and pictures

Trainer again presents designated picture and blank card saying: "Let's play with the _____ again. Look at the picture".

Does child look at the picture within 15 seconds?

no → Trainer removes pictures - recycle to 10 trials

yes
Trainer brings toy into view; plays with child and toy - 15 seconds

Recycle (10 trials)

yes

Trainer brings object into view and removes pictures. Trainer interacts with child and object for 15 seconds

Recycle to 10 trials

Recycle to 10 trials

FIGURE 5

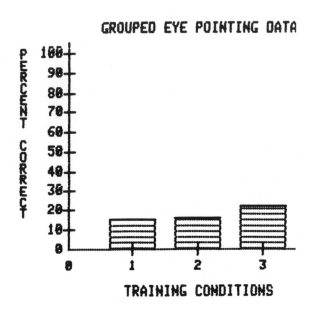

GROUPED EYE POINTING DATA

TRAINING CONDITIONS

training due to placement in a public school classroom. (However, this student was making gains through training as represented in Figure 6).

Student #2: This student showed a clear deceleration in performance under training conditions (Figure 7). Strong inference testing yielded a number of hypotheses, primary among which was the possibility that severe hypotonia with lack of head control in sitting (even when assisted by a soft cervical collar) might influence ocular motor control and subsequent ability to fixate on a picture for any length of time. This hypothesis was tested by using a two-choice discrimination paradigm where pictures were paired with either a blank distractor (training condition #2) or with colored pictures of objects/people (conditions #3-#9) (see Figure 9).

Data collected on communication behavior under these conditions differed from the eye pointing procedures in

FIGURE 6

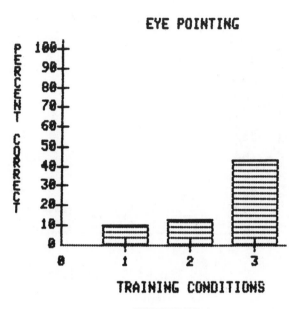

EYE POINTING

TRAINING CONDITIONS

STUDENT NO. 1

several ways. The training paradigm included supine (back lying) positioning on a slightly elevated wedge and required a head-turning response to either the right or the left with subsequent visual attention to the named picture. Pictures of this child's mother, father, and preferred objects were used in initial training. Eye pointing in sitting position using the previous procedures and with photographs of his mother and father were also probed in sitting using the same reinforcement conditions implemented in supine. Figure 8 indicates performance on pictures of mother/father in sitting and in supine positions.

Measurements of visual regard to pictures as a potential system for nonverbal communication indicated that this student was able to look at certain pictures when named and presented in a two-choice discrimination paradigm. Therefore, the individualized team determined that continued training should be provided with additional vocabulary in

FIGURE 7

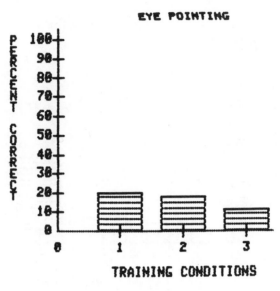

EYE POINTING

TRAINING CONDITIONS

STUDENT NO. 2

the supine position. As seen in Figure 9, conditions #5-#9 illustrate the sequence of activities attempted with this student. Initial pictures selected for visual attention included line drawings of a book and a drum which represented highly preferred activities (being read to from a book) and nonpreferred activities (beating a drum). When performance in head-turning and looking at the book in order to receive reinforcement of a story being read to the student by his mother (via a tape recording) was not above chance performance, the individualized team again implemented strong inference testing to determine if behavior was below chance performance because of lack of receptive language with respect to the book. Therefore, in condition #6, the book was always placed on the left hand side and the student was trained to head turn/look at book. In condition #7, book was paired with a blank distractor card and the two-choice discrimination paradigm was again used.

FIGURE 8

VISUAL DISCRIMINATION OF

MOTHER/FATHER PHOTOGRAPHS

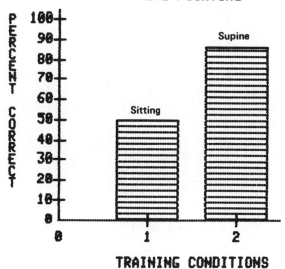

EYE POINTING

STUDENT NO. 2

Performance fell to chance levels again. The team then tested a hypothesis that the reason for this low performance was due to a line drawing rather than the photographs used in conditions #2, #3, and #4 by pairing a photograph of the book with a blank distractor in condition #8. When performance did not improve under these conditions, the team concluded that previous performance with book alone had trained left position rather than book. Current training (condition #9) includes pairing the picture of the book with a blank distractor and providing an aversive noise when response is to the incorrect side. Behavior is improving, under these conditions, indicating that this child can be taught the receptive vocabulary necessary for functional communication and a motor response of eye-pointing to a named picture.

FIGURE 9

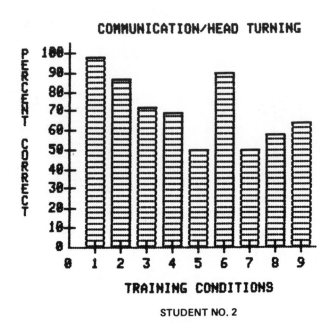

COMMUNICATION/HEAD TURNING

STUDENT NO. 2

Student #3: Little positive results have occurred as a function of attempting to train this child to eye-point to pictures for communication. However, the data have provided documentation which indicates that this student does not see pictures, objects, or line drawings. These data are remarkable in that this student is a multihandicapped 4-6 year old child who has had previous visual examinations which indicated potentially "poor visual acuity" but without a diagnosis of visual impairment.

Three different training strategies (conditions #4, #5, #6 on Figure 10) were attempted with this student following the implementation of initial training (condition #3). All four conditions of training resulted in increased performance above baseline (conditions #1 & #2). However, these gains were not significant and were relatively the same across all variances in training strategy. In training condition #4, the most visually attended to object across

FIGURE 10

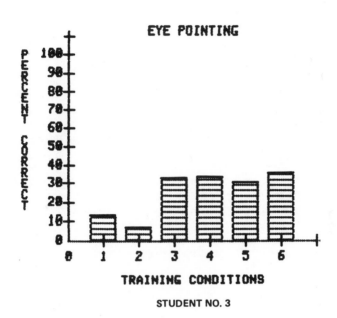

EYE POINTING

STUDENT NO. 3

baseline and initial training conditions (cup) was presented as a line drawing in a center position without any other stimulus present. The student was required to look at the cup to receive a sip of juice. When performance did not improve, attention was focused on the line drawing of cup by presenting the picture within a large box with controlled illumination of the line drawings. Five preferred line drawings were used which represented objects/toys identified as being "liked" by this student (condition #5). Again, performance did not substantially increase so team members suggested that perhaps this student required color in order to visually "see" the picture. To test this hypothesis, in addition to adding color to the pictures, stimuli were increased in size to 8"x10" photographs. Behavior did not improve. Subsequently, the procedure was altered in order to obtain visual attention to pictures in a back lying position. Data from this conditon more precisely defined visual conditions which could be used to elicit head-turn/ looking response. These conditions were defined as highly illumi-

nated and brightly colored stimuli presented <u>only</u> in a very
dark room. These data have been sent (with the student) to
an ophthalmologist in order to determine possible visual
corrective procedures which might be implemented for this
student.

   <u>Student #4</u>:   The training procedures, overall, have
been most effective with this student who has been diagnosed
as cortically blind! However, this child, like the other
three students, required a nonverbal communication system,
lacked voluntary movement, and was so severely handicapped
that staff decided to attempt visual programming despite the
diagnosis of visual impairment.

   Figure 11 shows the session-by-session data across all
training strategies attempted with this student. Although
the data indicate a slow acceleration curve with periodi-
cally variable performance, the student demonstrated acquisition of visual attention to a picture as well as some
(limited) evidence of generalization of attention to a non-

FIGURE 11

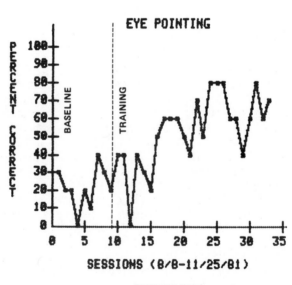

STUDENT NO. 4

trained stimulus. Figure #12 presents the same data grouped by training condition. Four different forms of training were identified and utilized with this student, again on the basis of team-generated strong inference testing. However, the hypotheses tested with this student related more directly to the characteristics of the visual antecedent(s) due to the previous diagnosis of cortical blindness.

In training condition #4, the team decided to train visual attention to the stimulus which received greatest visual regard by this student during baseline (preferred items) and initial training (condition #3) conditions. Data derived from previous functional vision assessments conducted with this student had indicated that color was a key characteristic related to visual acuity and that movement of the stimulus brought and maintained attention to the stimulus when placed close to the face. Therefore, a colored line-drawing of a smiling face (infant type) was used to train attention in condition #4. Verbal reinforcement was used as a consequence to attending for 3 second periods. Although performance improved above previous training efforts, the individualized team concluded that attention could be improved by restricting the number of visual stimuli. Therefore, similar procedures as were used with student #3 were implemented and the stimulus was presented within a box which limited the visual environment. In addition, the stimulus was moved to attract the attention of the student. Performance improved dramatically under these conditions (condition #5) of training. Therefore, the team concluded that movement of the stimulus was important in training but that further training would have to be implemented in order to fade the movement and bring the visual regard under the control of the picture (as the only antecedent stimulus). Movement was faded as a cue in training condition #6 and although performance levels fell somewhat, success remained at a level above previous conditions. A picture of his mother, consequated by his mother's voice providing the verbal reinforcement, was then simultaneously attempted while continuing to provide training with the smile face. Performance again remained high, possibly indicating some "transfer" of visual attention skills learned in relation to the smiling face stimulus (highly preferred) to another stimulus. Training is continuing by adding addi-

FIGURE 12

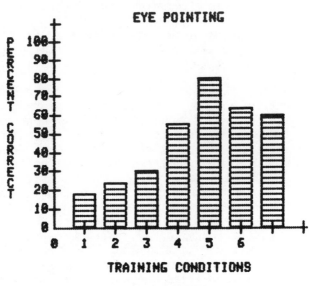

STUDENT NO. 4

tional visual stimuli that are more functional than the
highly preferred smiling face and where success can be
functionally consequated. However, data do indicate a
training progression that has been appropriate for and
effective in teaching this student to begin to be able to
use eye pointing as a means of nonverbal communication.

CONCLUSION

Team organizational structures of multidisciplinary,
interdisciplinary, and transdisciplinary models have been
suggested in the literature as beneficial methods for providing programming for handicapped individuals. More recently, the transdisciplinary model has been the most highly
advocated for use with young handicapped children or in
public education settings. None of the team organizational
structures is most effective in meeting the needs of handicapped young children. Rather, what is required is a model

that is based on the effectiveness of programming in changing the behavior of the handicapped child by teaching therapeutic and instructional skills with efficient and effective methods and techniques.

The individualized programming team model organizes individuals with different types of expertise (including the parents of the child) around the particular instructional and therapeutic needs of the child. Using test-teach, strong inference testing, and a theoretically sound intervention model, members of the individualized programming team can substantiate that intervention provided for each student has been effective in changing the behavior of the child. Initial programming goals are identified through parent interview, staff assessment, and test-teach approaches which allow the team constantly to monitor the appropriateness of what is being taught to the child. Regular data collection on child performance provides each member with objective data used to guide selection and evaluation of techniques implemented with individual students or groups of students.

Any model of team organization must "fit" the overall service delivery system in which that model is implemented. Some models will be more appropriate within specific service delivery systems. However, the individualized programming team is compatible with almost any type of service delivery system utilized with young children. Flexibility of organization and membership, based on sound theory and a focus on improving and documenting improvement in child performance, insures that team members will be maximally effective and efficient changers of young children's skill acquisition.

Acknowledgement:

Preparation of this article was funded in part from USOE/BEH Grant no. G00-79-00506 to Children's Hospital Medical Center of Akron.

REFERENCE NOTES

1.   APTA, Report on physical therapy services in public schools, May, 1981.

2. Bureau of Education for the Severely Handicapped.
    Second Annual Report to Congress on the Implementation
    of Public Law 94-142, 1980.

3. Campbell, P.H.   Application of management systems in
    early childhood education for special needs children.
    Report for WESTAR, March, 1981.

4. Keough, B., & Kopp, C.   From assessment to interven-
    tion: The elusive bridge.   Paper presented, Los
    Angeles, October, 1979.

REFERENCES

Albano, M. L., Cox, B., York, J., & York, R. Educational
    team for students with severe and multiple handicaps.
    In R. York, W. Schofield, D. J. Donder, & D. L. Ryndak
    (Eds.), The severely and profoundly handicapped child.
    Illinois: Illinois State Board of Education, 1981.

Beck, R. Interdisciplinary model: Planning distribution
    and ancillary input to classrooms for the severely/
    profoundly handicapped. In E. Sontag, N. Certo, & J.
    Smith (Eds.), Educational programming for the severely
    and profoundly handicapped. Reston, Virginia: Council
    for Exceptional Children, 1977.

Bell, P. Child-related stress in families of handicapped
    children. Topics in early childhood special education,
    1981, 3, 45-53.

Bricker, D. Educational synthesizer. In M. A. Thomas
    (Ed.), Hey, don't forget about me! Reston, Virginia:
    Council for Exceptional Children, 1976.

Bricker, D. A rationale for the integration of handicapped
    and nonhandicapped preschool children. In M. J. Gural-
    nick (Ed.), Early intervention and the integration of
    handicapped and nonhandicapped children.   Baltimore:
    University Park Press, 1978.

Bricker, W. A. Service of research. In M. A. Thomas (Ed.),
    Hey, don't forget about me! Reston, Virginia: Council
    for Exceptional Children, 1976.

Bricker, D., Sheehan, R., & Littman, D. Early Intervention: A plan for evaluating program impact. Monmouth, Oregon: WESTAR Series Paper #10, 1981.

Bricker, W. A., & Campbell, P. H. Interdisciplinary assessment and programming for multihandicapped students. In W. Sailor, B. Wilcox, & L. Brown (Eds.), Methods of instruction for severely handicapped students. Baltimore, Maryland: Paul H. Brookes, 1980.

Bromwich, R. Working with parents and infants. Baltimore, Maryland: University Park Press, 1981.

Bronfenbrenner, U. Is early intervention effective? In B. Z. Friedlander, G. M. Sterritt, & G. E. Kirk (Eds.), Exceptional infant. New York: Brunner/Mazel, 1975.

Caldwell, B. M. The importance of beginning early. In J. B. Jordan & R. F. Dailey (Eds.), Not all wagons are red: The exceptional child's early years. Arlington, Virginia: The Council for Exceptional Children, 1972.

Caldwell, B. M. The rationale for early intervention. Exceptional Children, 1970, Summer, 717-726.

Campbell, P. H. & Bricker, W. A. Programming for the severely handicapped person. In J. Gardner, L. Long, R. Nichols, & D. Iagulli (Eds.), Program issues in developmental disabilities. Baltimore: Paul H. Brookes Publishers, 1980.

Caputo, A. The efficacy of therapy in early intervention. AACP Newsletter, Summer, 1981.

Cohen, S., Semmes, M., & Guralnick, M. Public Law 94-142 and the education of preschool handicapped children. Exceptional Children, 1979, 45(4), 279-285.

Connor, F. P., Williamson, G. G., & Sieppe, J. M. Program guide for infants and toddlers with neuromotor and other developmental disabilities. New York: Teacher's College Press, 1978.

Denhoff, E. Current status of infant stimulation or enrichment programs for children with developmental disabilities. Pediatrics, 1981, 67, 32-37.

Garland, C., Stone, N. W., Swanson, J., & Woodruff, G.
Early intervention for children with special needs
and their families. Monmouth, Oregon: WESTAR Series
Paper #11, 1981.

Garwood, S. Early childhood special education: Issues for
the 1980s. Topics in Early Childhood Special Education, 1981, 1, viii-x.

Guralnick, M. J. Early intervention and the integration of
handicapped and nonhandicapped children. Baltimore:
University Park Press, 1978.

Haring, N. G., Liberty, K. A., & White, O. R. Rules for
data-based strategy decisions in instruction programs:
Current research and instructional implications. In W.
Sailor, B. Wilcox, and L. Brown (Eds.), Methods of
instruction for severely handicapped students. Baltimore: Paul H. Brookes Publishers, 1980.

Hart, V. The use of many disciplines with the severely and
profoundly handicapped. In E. Sontag, N. Certo, & J.
Smith (Eds.), Educational programming for the severely
and profoundly handicapped. Reston, Virginia: Council
for Exceptional Children, 1977.

Hayden, A. H. Handicapped children, birth to age 3. Exceptional Children, 1979, 45, 510-516.

Hobbs, N. The futures of children: Categories, labels, and
their consequences. The Jossey-Bass behavioral science
series. San Francisco: Jossey-Bass, 1975.

Horowitz, F. D., & Paden, L. Y. The effectiveness of environmental intervention programs. In B. M. Caldwell &
H. N. Ricciuti (Eds.), Child development research.
Chicago, Illinois: The University of Chicago Press,
1973.

Hutchinson, D. J. The transdisciplinary approach. In J. B.
Curry & K. K. Peppe (Eds.), Mental retardation: Nur-
sing approaches to care. St. Louis: C. V. Mosby Co.,
1978.

Keough, B. K. Early detection of learning problems: Questions, cautions, and guidelines, Exceptional Children, 1973, 40, 5-11.

Lyon, S., & Lyon, G. Team functioning and staff development: A role release approach to providing integrated educational services for severely handicapped students. Journal of the Association for the Severely Handicapped, 1980, 5(3), 250-263.

Orlando, C. Multidisciplinary team approaches in the assessment of handicapped preschool children. Topics in Early Childhood Special Education, 1981, 2, 23-30.

Peterson, C. P. Support services. In B. Wilcox & R. York (Eds.), Quality education for the severely handicapped. Washington, D.C.: U.S. Department of Education, 1980.

Safford, P. L. Teaching young children with special needs. St. Louis: The C. V. Mosby Company, 1978.

Sternat, J., Messina, R., Nietupski, J., Lyon, S., & Brown, L. Occupational and physical therapy services for severely handicapped students: Toward a naturalized public school service delivery model. In E. Sontag, N. Certo, & J. Smith (Eds.), Educational programming for the severely and profoundly handicapped.   Reston, Virginia: Council for Exceptional Children, 1977.

Swan, W. W. The handicapped children's early education program. Exceptional Children, 1980, 47, (1), 12-16.

Tjossem, T. D. (Ed.), Intervention strategies for high risk infants and young children. Baltimore: University Park Press, 1976.

Turnbull, A. P. & Blacher-Dixon, J. Preschool mainstreaming: Impact on parents. In J. J. Gallagher (Ed.), New directions for exceptional children. San Francisco: Jossey-Bass, Inc., 1980.

Vincent, L. J., & Broome, K. A pubic school service delivery model for handicapped children between birth and five years of age. In E. Sontag, N. Certo, & J. Smith (Eds.), Educational programming for the severely and profoundly handicapped. Reston, Virginia: Council for Exceptional Children, 1977.

Vincent, L. J., Salisbury, C., Walter, G., Brown, P., Gruen-
    wald, L. J., & Powers, M. Program evaluation and
    curriculum   development   in   early   childhood/special
    education: Criteria of the next environment.   In W.
    Sailor, B. Wilcox, & L. Brown (Eds.), Methods of in-
    struction for severely handicapped students.   Balti-
    more: Paul H. Brookes Publishers, 1980.

7

MODEL TRAINING PROGRAMS FOR PARENTS
OF HANDICAPPED INFANTS AND CHILDREN

Nicholas J. Anastasiow
Hunter College, New York

The parent not the child is the focus of this chapter.
This does not mean to imply that the child is not the object
of concern; rather the intent is to highlight that the
parent or primary caregiver is the natural and necessary
facilitator of the child's development. Programs that
involve or train parents intend their services to flow
through the parent to the child. The sections that follow
present a brief review of the rationale and research literature that has directed current programming for parents. The
first section summarizes the effects of the environment on
development, the impact of experience in the early years,
and the role of the parent in facilitating development. An
examination of early parent programs will then be made,
followed by guidelines for establishing programs to meet the
special needs of parents of handicapped children.

Experience and Development

In the early 1960s, Hunt's book _Intelligence and Exper-
ience_ (1961) led to a major rethinking of the concepts of
fixed intelligence and the role of environmental experiences
on human development. Hunt was impressed with the work of
Skeels (1966) and Skeels and Dye (1939) concerning the
impact on adult performance of both adoption and low child-
to-adult ratio in institutional settings. Spitz (1946) and
Bowlby (1960) addressed the problem as maternal deprivation
and associated the separation of mother and child during the
infancy period with many infant deaths and with delayed
development and below normal IQ scores.

The work of Skeels and Dye (1939) demonstrated that
infants in orphanages who were reared on an individual basis
by mentally retarded adults fared better than infants reared
by one nurse to 15 or more infants. Further, children who
were placed out for adoption tended to live normal lives as
adults, whereas infants who remained in institutions rarely
escaped the institution and functioned at lower intellectual
and occupational levels as adults.

87

Hunt's work not only highlighted these previous studies but also legitimatized Piagetian (1970) theory into American psychology. At the core of Piagetian theory is the notion of the importance of the environment in transacting with what is genetically available for full development. To Piaget (1970), low functioning can be a product of a lack of experience as well as genetic factors. While it is not always stated, it is important to note that it is the care-giver in the environment who does or does not provide the enriched environmental experiences.

Not all American psychologists were ready to accept Skeels and Dye's or Piaget's work. The statistically oriented methodologists tended to reject Piaget's studies of his three children as not meeting the scientific rigor of randomly-assigned comparison groups. Further Skeels and Dye's study failed to explain or describe what happened in adoptive family environments that resulted in higher IQ scores for the adopted children.

Nonetheless, Hunt's work sparked a chord in society, and programs such as Head Start and Homestart can be seen as results of a renewed interest in environmental events on normal functioning. These innovative programs of the 1960s stressed that the causes of lower achievement patterns of the poor were due not to poor genes but to lack of environ-mental stimulation. In the ensuing decade, not all re-searchers agreed with this point of view; the opposing arguments have been summarized elsewhere (Anastasiow and Hanes, 1976; Ginsburg, 1972). This overview will summarize positive results regarding environmental stimulation. Specifically, three types of research will be reviewed: animal studies on the impact of environmental enrichment, longitudinal studies on the impact of the environment, and studies of the impact of social intervention programs on academic and social achievements.

The Evidence

Animal researchers provided evidence along a number of dimensions to dramatically demonstrate the impact of an enriched environment on the course of an animal's develop-ment. These results were so widespread as to be taken as truisms in animal development. Animals raised in enriched environments, in contrast to those who were not free to roam and play in an enriched environment, have heavier cortices, more synaptic connections among neurons, enriched dendritic treeing on neurons, and greater skill in learning experimentally-derived problems (Chall and Mirsky, 1978; Walsh and Greenough, 1976). Further, experience has been demonstrated to be necessary in learning to walk and see, and it also assists in recovery from experimentally-produced brain damage (Will, Rosenzweig, Bennett, Herbert, & Morimoto, 1977). The converse, the impact of a limiting or deprived environment, can lead to a variety of debilitating physical, cognitive, and emotional disorders (Walsh and Greenough, 1976). Animal research also demonstrates that the impact of experience is strongest during infancy when the brain has not reached full maturation.

It is difficult to demonstrate equivalent findings with humans due to moral constraints in conducting similar experiments. An analogy can be found, however, in the impact of early experience on two sensory disorders: blindness and deafness. The untreated blind infant is likely to develop stereotypic body swaying and autistic-like behaviors (Barraga, 1971; Fraiberg, 1977). If, however, extra physical stimulation is provided during the first 7 months of life to offset the visual deficit, these abnormal behaviors do not appear. Similarly, deaf youngsters do not develop the grimacing and hollow speech usually associated with deafness if intervention is begun before two years of age (Horton, 1974). More broad-scale findings have been found as a result of early childhood programs for the handicapped (DeWeerd, 1974; Wynne, Ulfelder, and Dakof, 1975). Handicapped children who participate in early childhood programs make significantly greater gains in cognitive, social, and physical development than handicapped children who did not participate in such programs. It is of particular importance that handicapped children make even greater gains if the program includes training for parents (Stedman, 1972).

In addition, several longitudinal studies have demonstrated that the best predictors of a child's IQ, verbal scores, school achievement, and adult functioning, are the level of the mother's education (Broman, Nichols, and Kennedy, 1975), the quality of care in the home during the first year of life (Neligan, Prudham, and Steiner, 1974), the nature of the caretaking environment (Elardo, Bradley, and Caldwell, 1975, 1977), and the nature of the mother's parenting style (Werner, Bierman, and French, 1971; Werner and Smith, 1977, 1981). These findings have been summarized more extensively elsewhere (Anastasiow, 1981a).

Not only do the parenting skills have impact on normal development, but they can do much to offset certain forms of high risk conditions occurring at birth, such as anoxia (Sameroff, 1979), malnutrition (Richardson, 1976) and a host of potential problems associated with low birthweight and prematurity (Werner and Smith, 1981). The results of these studies emphasize the importance of the caretaking environment during the first two years of life when the infant is undergoing major maturation of the brain and associated brain systems.

The last line of evidence comes from research on the impact of social intervention programs. The studies of Head Start, Homestart, and other early intervention programs demonstrate a variety of socially desirable results (Lazar, Hubbell, Murray, Rosche & Royce, 1977; Schwienhart and Weikart, 1980). Children who have experienced early intervention are more committed to schooling, are less delinquent, have higher self-concepts and social development, spend less time in special education classes and are less often retained in grade. Further, in two major studies in which economically-deprived infants were provided an enriched environment from birth, all the children who were so exposed obtained normal IQs and high verbal functioning, whereas, the untreated comparison group did not (Garber and Heber, 1976; Hunt, 1976).

The generalization to be drawn from this evidence is that the caregiving environment and styles of parenting influence both the rate and outcome of development and, further, help reduce or offset the negative impact of handicapping conditions. Programs designed to modify the environment and to enhance the parents' adoption of facilitating childrearing strategies can do much to favorably affect the child's life. If the child has a sensory impairment or other handicapping condition, parent training is an effective means of assisting the child (Karnes, 1970; Lillie, 1981; Lillie and Trohanis, 1976).

Early Impact and Studies of Parent Training

There are several excellent general summaries of the results of programs designed to either train or involve parents (Bronfenbrenner, 1975; Goodson and Hess, 1975; Hanes, Gordon, and Breivogel, 1976; Lillie and Trohanis, 1976; Peters, 1977; Stedman, et al., 1972; Wiegerink and Parrish, 1975). Only some of the highlights of these works are represented here.

First, clarification of the term involvement is necessary. Programs that were designed to assist handicapped children involved the parents in a variety of ways. In some programs, the parents were involved as members of an advisory board. In a loose sense, they react to policy decision and, in some cases, assist in setting policy. In other programs, parents became essential sources of dissemination of information to other parents or to community decision-makers. Parents were trained to be advocates. The information interchange between parent and professional was then taken by the parent for further dissemination of the professional knowledge. Another model trained parents as aides to assist in the intervention program. Parents often performed low-level tasks, such as preparing snacks, assisting in toilet training, and other necessary but nonprofessional duties. In still another design, the parents were the focus of the program and were trained to be the teachers of their own children. In these programs, the professionals modeled their techniques and systematically taught the parents how to provide the necessary stimulation or remediation for their children.

A report by Gordon (1975) suggested that there were three major categories of programs designed for working with parents. The first included programs that visited the home. These programs were suited to rural areas where it was difficult for parents to take their children long distances to a center. The Portage project (Shearer and Shearer, 1976) in Wisconsin was an excellent example of a home-based model in which the home visitor provided the parent with activities to be carried out with the child.

Another type of program allowed professional staff to work with parents in the center in which the child received treatment. There were three·subtypes in this category. In the first, the parent activity consisted of parent group meetings in which discussions usually centered around the needs of handicapped children and their parents. The second subtype included direct parent interaction with the child in the center. The SPIN project in north Philadelphia was an excellent sample. In this project, parent meetings were held on Saturday morning when both parents could attend. During the morning, the parents had time for group discussion to share their needs as parents of handicapped children. Following this personal time, the parents were trained to work with their children. Included in this training were motor exercises taught by physical therapists, since many physically-disabled infants were enrolled in the SPIN program. (Losinno, note 1)

The third subtype involved a center program for children in which the parents observed. In some cases, the parents not only observed but were also taught how to work with their children. An example of one type of center plus parent-training-in-center was Northcott's (1972) program. This program, designed for hearing-impaired toddlers, provided habilitative exercises and a variety of general preschool play activities. On occasions, mothers were trained by a therapist in a special classroom set up like a kitchen in a regular home. The therapist demonstrated how to interact with a deaf child while cooking as the child's mother videotaped the experience. The child then left the classroom and the therapist and mother analyzed the tape noting the techniques used. In the following session, the child and his mother prepared something in the kitchen while the therapist videotaped the lesson. The therapist and mother critiqued the tape after the child returned to the classroom.

Research reports by Hanes, et al. (1976) and Peters (1977) suggest that the training programs that focused on the parent as teacher tended to have the most positive gains for the child. Greater gains were made when the program was highly structured, had a well planned curriculum, and stressed cognitive development. Not only were there positive changes for the child, but also parents experienced benefits in that those trained became more responsive, sensitive, and relaxed.

These program benefits to familes were widespread. Program staff helped the family understand the handicapped child's strengths and weaknesses, as well as what could be expected in the future. By modeling stimulation strategies, staff demonstrated how to encourage development in the impaired child. The outcome was increased skill and knowledge regarding handicapping conditions and cognitive gains in general, particularly as they pertained to infant and child development.

Program staff were able to assist parents in obtaining needed resources. Too often low social class parents of a handicapped child are unaware of how to seek resources across agencies. If the parent happens to contact a health agency, the services obtained will be primarily health-oriented and may not include educational services. Staff could then assist the family in finding help over a wide set of service agencies.

As more and more early childhood educators became parent educators, it became apparent that working with only the child was inadequate. Rather, what was needed was a staff member who focused on the total family needs and the problems associated with having a handicapped child.

Needs of Parents of Handicapped Children

To those who worked with parents of handicapped children, it became increasingly clear that these parents have special needs. Their needs range from emotional, economic and social, to training in remediational techniques. The emotional needs of handicapped parents are often so overwhelming they must be dealt with immediately by a professional trained in counseling techniques. Excellent advice on how to proceed with parents is available in Enzer (1976); Enzer, Abid, and Benaderet (1978); Lillie (1981); Linder (note 2); Morrison (1978); Simeonsson and Simeonsson (1981). The following is abstracted from their descriptions.

The first issue to be dealt with is the loss of self-esteem and the shame associated with having a handicapped child. There may be actual or perceived social ambivalence or rejection. There is often anger, depression, and grief, much as there is in mourning a death. These parents frequently feel isolated by society. In addition, they feel a loss of control over their lives in the face of the child's continuous needs for medical care, diagnostic sessions, treatments, prosthetic devices, and other special care.

Linder (note 2) suggests that parents search for a cause, then search for a solution. In addition, although they may finally accept that their child is handicapped, parents of handicapped children are subject to recurring feelings of depression, guilt, and anger.

Thus, the parent of a handicapped child has to learn not only how to be an effective parent but also how to cope with the special problems of facilitating the growth and meeting the special needs of the handicapped child. In addition, the parent must know how to secure economic resources and assistance from community agencies designed to provide support and services. Increasingly, those who work with parents of handicapped children are viewing the family as a complex system rather than as individuals who need to know how to train a handicapped child (Linder, note 2; Morrison, 1978; Paul, 1981; Selig, 1977).

The Family as a System

A systems approach to understanding the family attempts to determine the stages of a family's development. Families are perceived as two individuals who come together to make a commitment to each other and to reduce their commitment to the family of their parents. As the family develops, nurturance and support are provided by the couple. This in turn leads to a higher level of family involvement in which the individuals become more autonomous while still relying upon the nurturance of the system. Finally, the family system can assist its members in attaining actualization much in the sense implied by Maslow (1970).

Family-system workers suggest that the level of family functioning should be asssessed before any intervention is attempted. In Colorado, the Parent Encouraging Parents (PEP) program has initiated a major effort in assisting parents of handicapped children. The State Department of Special Education brings together groups of parents of handicapped children for a two day workshop. The intentions of the program are to assist parents in working through their emotional problems associated with having a handicapped child, to provide them with information as to the legal rights for their child and where they might find the services they need.

The goals of PEP are stated as:

1. PEP will provide support to parents of handi-capped children with emphasis on emotional support to those parents of newly identified handicapped children. Support will consist of a) personal contact in order to share experiences and develop a common bond, and b) accompanying parents to staffings upon request in order to support and alleviate anxieties.

2. PEP will provide an information system to parents of handicapped children which will make available human and material resources with regard to the Colorado Special Education Process, current legislation, due process and administrative appeal and characteristics of services to meet children's needs.

3. PEP will provide a communication link between parents and administrators in order to facil-itate open communication and good public relations.

4. PEP will provide a system of crisis preven-tion by facilitating, upon request, communi-cation to reconcile differences through mediation and negotiation before crisis situations occur.

5. PEP will provide a state wide resource system to parents of similarly handicapped children by disseminating a Parent Volunteer Resource List of parents with children having specific categorical handicaps.

6. PEP will provide consistent parent education through state, regional and local workshops and periodic dissemination of current litera-ture and information.

7.   PEP will function strictly as a support
     system and not as a political lever by
     sharing information and experience to help
     parents of handicapped children (Amens,
     Parents Encouraging Parents, Colorado Depart-
     ment of Education, Special Education Ser-
     vices, 1980).

Parents are encouraged to recognize their common problems associated with grief, denial, anger and eventually
acceptance. In addition, parents' viewpoints towards professionals and administrators are discussed as well as
viewpoints of the administrator. The result is a breakdown
of the isolation of the parent of a handicapped child as
well as enhanced information and emotional support.

The same group of parents is invited back at a later
time after the initial workshop to a values-clarification
workshop. The goal of this second level meeting is to
explore common problems and to invent solutions while improving communication skills of parents with professionals.
The results have been encouraging as the parents are forming
support systems and have sought solutions to their needs as
well as to their child's needs outside of litigation.

In an effort to reduce handicapping conditions, the
next largest group of parents being educated after parents
of handicapped children, is adolescent parents. The growing
number of young girls under 16 years of age who bear children has resulted in a number of programs designed to teach
young people how to facilitate their infant's development.
Two approaches will be examined next. For a more complete
review of programs for teenage parents, see Anastasiow
(1981b).

Parent Programs for Teens

According to the longitudinal studies, over the past
three decades the bulk of the middle class has adopted
childrearing attitudes that are facilitative to their
child's development. The lower class, however, regardless
of race or ethnic group, tends to hold less facilitative
attitudes. Given that parenting attitudes and childrearing
practices are passed on by the family (Papajohn and Speigel,
1975), these nonfacilitating attitudes will persist unless

direct training is instituted. Many schools provide some
instruction in child development, but usually at the high
school level and in classes attended mainly by girls
(Anastasiow, 1981b). As desirable as these courses are,
they are not reaching young girls who become pregnant and
drop out of school before they have had the course. The
fate of these girls is bleak. They remain unmarried or are
divorced, on welfare and unemployable. Frequently they are
in poor health and are malnourished. They are likely to
bear a second child within a year. Among the very young
(10-12 years old), the risk of bearing a low birthweight,
premature, and/or handicapped child is high. About 96% of
these young mothers keep their babies resulting in approximately 1.3 million children living with pre-teen parents in
1978 (Alan Guttmacher Institute, 1981). Given that many of
these young parents do not know how to offset stress factors
and how to encourage their infant's development, it can be
anticipated that without intervention the schools will see
an increase in the number of low-functioning and handicapped
children.

Many types of programs have been designed to deal with
some aspect of this problem. Three types will be discussed
here. The first, designed to reach adolescents in general;
the second, designed to deal with the teen mother and her
infant; and the third, designed to reach all teens before
they have children.

The Educational Development Corporation (EDC) has
developed a program called Exploring Childhood (Morris,
1977). It contains comprehensive materials in a multimedia
package designed for high school students. There are over
5,000 classes currently under way in the United States. In
addition, there have been allied programs conducted by the
Boy Scouts, Girl Scouts, 4-H, and the Salvation Army. In
addition to presenting information about child growth and
development, these programs attempt to provide a direct
experience with children. The experiences are usually in a
kindergarten or nursery school. In some cases, the childen
enrolled in the preschool classes are the children of the
teenage students. The EDC Exploring Childhood and other
allied programs have reported significant but small gains in
knowledge of child development. Greater gains have been
measured in the participants' attitudes toward their children.

There are many programs designed for the adolescent girl who is pregnant or has just delivered. Badger (1971) designed a program for the adolescent mother to be implemented in a hospital setting after the birth of the child. Badger and her staff contact the teenage mother shortly after delivery in an attempt to enroll the mother and infant in a series of weekly classes lasting until the baby is 6 months old. Badger's curriculum includes information on child development, nutrition, health, and infant stimulation. Staff members model ways of interacting with the infant and help the mother to determine signs of the infant's vocalizations that indicate distress, hunger, or comfort. The mothers are taught also appropriate play strategies to encourage their infant's development, as well as a variety of child care and home management techniques.

The results of the program have been encouraging. Two-thirds of the graduates of the program became employed. The babies of these program participants have normal IQs as compared to an average IQ of 79 for an untreated group. The mothers who participated in the program have tended not to have the second child within the following year and some have gone on to finish high school.

The last program to be discussed is Facilitating Environments Encouraging Development (FEED). Unlike most so-called parenting programs, FEED is designed for all students and is aimed at the 12- to 13-year-old. The basic experience is a course in child development combined with three practicum experiences. The in-class experience deals with principles of child development presented through multimedia materials, discussions and lectures all tied to objectives outlined in the guidelines.

Practicum experiences provided in FEED include working with preschool normal and handicapped children and working in a health care facility. The practicum experiences provide direct experience with and observation of normal and abnormal development. They contain a wide set of direct encounters with serious health and behavioral problems. In New York City, the students have worked in a preschool setting for seriously handicapped children. They have learned how to sign, to provide auditory and visual stimulation to a legally blind and deaf rubella victim, to assist physically disabled children to walk, to teach impaired children to feed themselves and to deal with the death of a damaged child who was the product of a teenage birth. The hospital experience includes reading to and playing with long-term surgery patients or abandoned damaged infants who need human stimulation to survive. The students assist in wheeling patients out of their rooms into a group playroom to provide more normal interaction than can be provided in the hospital room.

The program is based on the concept that attitudes are difficult to change and can best be influenced by direct encounters. Once students have experience with handicapped children of teenage mothers, these 12- and 13-year-olds become vocal about the irresponsibility of teenage births.

The results of FEED have been encouraging. Students who participate hold more positive attitudes toward normal and handicapped infants and children and in some sites are less fearful of hospitals and adults. Participants have detected and referred delayed children to centers in their community, have volunteered to work in preschool handicapped or Head Start programs without pay, and in one community, have dominated the ranks of Candy Stripers. Interviews with students and the professionals with whom they work attest to the positive gains these students make. The program is more completely described in two guides available from Educational Development Corporation.

Summary and Conclusions

Current evidence suggest that environmental enrichment is important for development, particularly during infancy. Further, the manner in which the environment is structured by the primary caregiver influences the outcome of children's measured IQ and their language development. The utilization of good verbal models, warmth, low physical punishment, and a push for achievement does much to insure that normal infants become normal adults and in some cases facilitates stressed infants' attainment of normalcy.

Special services are needed to help parents deal with the emotional problems associated with bearing a handicapped child. Other parents of handicapped children can do much to assist. For lower class and adolescent parents, continued efforts are needed to assist them in learning about and adopting facilitative childrearing techniques. Many models are currently available but more need to be created.

There are 1,187,000 handicapped children in the United States and only 38% are being served. In addition, the 554,000 yearly teenage births will contribute more new handicapped children to the total.

Involving parents in learning how to assist their children in attaining normal functioning by the time they reach elementary school age is seen as an important way of meeting a wide set of societal goals. The quality of life for all of us would seem to depend upon how successfully this goal will be accomplished in the future.

REFERENCE NOTES

1.   Losinno, D.A. SPIN (Write: David A. Lossino, Special People in the N.E., 8040 Roosevelt Blvd., Room 219, Philadelphia, PA. 19152).

2.   Linder, T. Developing early childhood special education programs (in preparation).

REFERENCES

Alan Guttmacher Institute. Teenage pregnancy: The problem that hasn't gone away. New York: The Alan Guttmacher Institute, 1981.

Amens, C. Parents encouraging parents (PEP). Denver, Colorado: Department of Education, Special Education Services, 1980.

Anastasiow, N.J. Two views of early childhood education. In: R. Wiegerink, et al. (Eds.). A review of early childhood services for children with developmental disabilities and their families. National Review of Child Developmental Services Project: A State of the Art, 1981a (In press).

Anastasiow, N.J. Preparing adolescents in childrearing: Before and after pregnancy. In: M. Sugar (Ed.). Adolescent Parenthood. New York: Spectrum, 1981b.

Anastasiow, N.J., & Hanes, M.L. Language patterns of poverty children. Springfield: Charles C. Thomas, 1976.

Badger, E. Infant and toddler learning programs. McGraw-Hill Early Learning. Paoli, Pa. Instructo Corporation, 1971.

Barraga, N. Visual handicaps and learnings. Belmont: Wadsworth, 1971.

Bowlby, J. Separation anxiety. International Journal of Pscyhoanalysis, 1960, 41, 80-113.

Broman, S.H., Nichols, P.L., & Kennedy, W.A. Preschool I.Q.. Hillsdale: Lawrence Erlbaum Associates, 1975.

Bronfenbrenner, U. Is early intervention effective? In: J. Hellmuth (Ed.). Exceptional infants - Vol. III. New York: Bruner/Mazel, 1975.

Chall, J.S. & Mirsky, A.F. Education and the brain. Chicago: University of Chicago Press, 1978.

DeWeerd, J. Federal programs for the handicapped. Exceptional Children, 1974, 40(6), 441.

Elardo, R., Bradley, R., & Caldwell, B.N. The relation of infants' home environments to mental tests performance from six to thirty six months: A longitudinal analysis. Child Development, 1975, 46, 71-76.

Elardo, R., Bradley, R., & Caldwell, B.N. A longitudinal study of the relation of infants' home environment to language development at age three. Child Development, 1977, 48, 595-603.

Enzer, N. Parent-child and professional interaction. In: D.L. Lillie and P.L. Trohanis (Eds.). Teaching parents to teach, pp. 17-31. New York: Walker and Company, 1976.

Enzer, N.B., Abid, N. Jr., & Benaderet, L.B. Treatment of preschool children: An overview. In: Social and emotional development: The preschooler, pp. 97-113. New York: Walker and Company, 1978.

Fraiberg, S. Insights from the blind. New York: Basic Books, 1977.

Garber, H., & Heber, T. the Milwaukee project: Indications of the effectiveness of early intervention to prevent mental retardation. In: P. Mittler (Ed.). Research to practice in mental retardation, Vol. I: Care and intervention. Baltimore: University Park ress, 1976.

Ginsberg, H. The myth of the deprived child. Englewood Cliffs: Prentice Hall, 1972.

Goodson, B.D., & Hess, R.D. Parents as teachers of young children: An evaluative review of some contemporary concepts and programs. Stanford: Stanford University Press, 1975.

Gordon, I.J. Parent oriented home-based early childhood education programs: A decision oriented review. Institute for Development of Human Resources, College of Education, University of Florida, Gainesville, 1975.

Hanes, M., Gordon, I., & Breivogel, W. (Eds). Update: The first 10 years of life. Proceedings from the conference celebrating the 10th anniversary of the Institute for Development of Human Resources, College of Education, University of Florida, Gainesville, 1976.

Horton, K.B. Infant intervention and language learning. In: L.R. Schiefelbusch and L.L. Lloyd (Eds.). Language perspectives, acquisition, retardation, and intervention. Baltimore: University Park Press, 1974.

Hunt, J. Experience and intelligence. New York: Ronald Press, 1961.

Hunt, J.M. Environmental programming to foster competence and prevent mental retardation in infancy. In: R.N. Walsh and W.T. Greenough (Eds.). Environments as therapy for brain dysfunction, Vol. 17: Advances in behavioral biology. New York: Plenum Press, 1976.

Karnes, M.B. Educational intervention at home by mothers of disadvantaged infants. Child Development, 1970, 41, 925-935.

Lazar, I., Hubbell, V.R., Murray, H., Rosche, M., and Royce, J. The persistence of preschool effects. Washington, D.C.: DHEW (OHDS) 78-30129, 1977.

Lillie, D. Educational and psychological strategies for working with parents. In: J.L. Paul (Ed.). Understanding and working with parents of children with special needs, pp. 89-118. New York: Holt, Rinehart and Winston, 1981.

Lillie, D.L. & Trohanis, P.L. (Eds.). Teaching parents to teach. New York: Walker and Company, 1976.

Maslow, A.H. Motivation and personality, second edition. New York: Harper and Row, 1970.

Morris, L.A. (Ed.). Education for parenthood: A program curriculum and evaluation guide. Washington, D.C.: DHEW (OHDS) 77-30125 1977.

Morrison, G.S. Parent involvement in the home, school, and community. Columbus: Charles E. Merrill, 1978.

Neligan, G., Prudham, D., & Steiner, H. Formative years: Birth, family and development in Newcastle upon Thames. London: Oxford University Press, 1974.

Northcott, W.H. Curriculum guide: Hearing impaired children (0-3 years) and their parents. Washington, D.C.: Alexander Graham Bell Association for the Deaf, 1972.

Papajohn, J., & Speigel, J. Transactions in families. San Francisco: Jossey-Bass, 1975.

Paul, J.L. (Ed.). Understanding and working with parents of children with special needs. New York: Holt, Rinehart, and Winston, 1981.

Peters, D.L. Early childhood education: An overview and Evaluation. In: H.L. Horn, Jr. and P.A. Robinson (Eds.). Psychological processes in early education. New York: Academic Press, 1977.

Richardson, S.A. The influence of severe malnutrition in infancy on the intelligence of children at school age: An ecological perspective. In: R.N. Walsh & W.T. Greenough (Eds.). Environments as therapy for brain dysfunction: Advances in behavioral biology, Vol. 17, New York: Plenum Press, 1976.

Sameroff, A.J. The etiology of cognitive competence: A systems perspective. In: R.B. Kearsley and I.E. Sigel (Eds.). Infants at risk: Assessment of cognitive functioning, pp. 115-151. Hillsdale: Earlbaum Associates, 1979.

Schweinhart, L., & Weitart, D. Effects of early childhood intervention on teenage youths. High Scope Monographs, 1980.

Selig, A.L. Making things happen in communities: Alternatives to traditional mental health services. San Francisco: R&E Research Associates, Inc., 1977.

Shearer, D., & Shearer, M.   A home-based parent-training model.   In: D Lillie & P. Trohanis (Eds.).   Teaching parents to teach.   New York: Walker and Co., 1976.

Simeonsson, R.J., & Simeonsson, N.E.   Parenting handicapped children: Psychological Aspects.   In: J.L. Paul (Ed.).   Understanding and working with parents of children with special needs, pp. 51-88.   New York: Holt, Rinehart, and Winston, 1981.

Skeels, H.M.   Adult status of children with contrasting early life experience.   Monograph Society for Research in Child Development, 1966, 31 (3).

Skeels, H.M., & Dye, H.B.   A study of the effects of different stimulation of mentally retarded children.   Proc. Amer. on Mental Deficiency, 1939, 44, 114-136.

Spitz, R.A.   Anaclitic depression.   Psychoanalytic Study of Children, 1946, 2, 313-342.

Stedman, D.J.   How can effective early intervention programs be delivered to potentially retarded children?   A report for the Office of the Secretary of the Department of DHEW, October, 1972.

Walsh, R.N. & Greenough, W.T.   Environments as therapy for brain dysfunction, Vol. 17:   Advances in behavioral biology.   New York: Plenum Press, 1976.

Werner, E.E., Bierman, J.M., & French, F.E.   The children of Kauai.   Honolulu: University Press of Hawaii, 1971.

Werner, E.E., & Smith, R.S.   Kauai's children come of age.   Honolulu: University of Hawaii, 1977.

Werner, E.E., & Smith, R.S.   Vulnerable, but invincible: A longitudinal study of resilient children and youth.   New York: McGraw-Hill, 1981.

Wiegerink, R., & Parrish, V.   A parent-implemented preschool program.   In: D.L. Lillie and P.L. Trohanis (Eds.).   Training parents to teach.   New York: Walker and Company, 1975.

Will, B.E., Rosenzweig, M.R., Bennett, E.L., Herbert, M. & Morimoto, H. Relatively brief environmental enrichment aids recovery of learning capacity and alters brain measures after postweaning brain lesions in rats. Journal of Comparative and Physiological Psychology, 1977, 91, (1), 33-50.

Wynne, S., Ulfelder, L.S. & Dakof, G. Mainstreaming and early childhood education for handicapped children: Review and implications of research. Washington, D.C.: DHEW (#OEC-74-9056), 1975.

Index